Gardening For The Complete Beginner

Contents

INTRODUCTION

WHAT IS GARDENING?

TYPES OF HOME GARDENS

TYPES OF FLORAL GARDENS

STARTING A GARDEN

HOW TO CHOOSE PLANTS AND SEEDLINGS FOR YOUR VERY OWN GARDEN

PLANT PARTNERS

ORGANIC GARDENING

COMPOSTING

MULCHING

URBAN GARDENING

TIPS ON PLANTING A GARDEN AT HOME

GARDEN MAINTENANCE AND PRUNING

GROWING YOUR OWN FOOD

FRUITS AND FLOWERS BY SEASON

TIPS ON STARTING A HOME GARDENING BUSINESS

MARKETING STRATEGIES YOU CAN USE FOR YOUR MICRO-FARM BUSINESS

RESOURCES FOR GARDENING

GARDENING AND HOW IT HELPS WITH MENTAL HEALTH, MINDFULNESS AND MEDITATION

FAQS ON GARDENING

CONCLUSION

RESOURCES

Introduction

Many people today are now trying their hand at gardening. It goes the same for me, the author. It's an enjoyable hobby and by far I have saved money on the food bill, and have my palates for a sweet ride with the freshly harvested food from my garden. I have been researching and practicing the principles and concepts about different kinds of gardening for years now. I grew up around plants, gardening and farming as it was our family's business and primary form of hobby and relaxation from my grandparents, my parents, aunts and uncles and now, down to me. I have successfully grown vegetables that we consume at home and even came up with a very simple yet packed with flavors recipe for salad dressing.

I was not always into gardening. For the first years of my working life, I was part of the "grind" club, where it was all about the hustle. The more hours put in, the more successful you will be. Don't get me wrong, this is very true. My career pays me on an hourly basis, so that means the more hours I put in, the more money I make. This work principle got me the material things the society defines as "tokens" of success, but has not helped with feeling at peace. This is when gardening came into play. By having this mindful experience, and working with my hands and with nature, little by little I was able to feel fulfilled with growing the vegetables I'm able to produce. There too, is a sense of accomplishment, and this I want to share with you and I'm sure you'll love it!

This book will walk you through the processes of breaking down and setting up a garden. You'll learn about the different types of plants and ways to care of your garden with basic and general knowledge that will get you started with gardening. I hope you'll find that you enjoy it as much as I do!

What is Gardening?

Gardening is one of the most accessible and fulfilling hobbies. You can do this practically anywhere, with minimal start up and equipment cost. The things you grow will not only help your health, it can also become a rich source of income, and gift baskets too! Not to mention how therapeutic tending to a garden can be – I'm confident that you'll love it. It is done in steps, therefore it's not a hobby for immediate gratification. You won't grow a garden from seed to harvest in a day. It's a slow and rewarding process of growing and nurturing. This book however will help you understand the basics of gardening and provide you with all the resources needed to get started!

Gardening, specifically the act of working in the garden, has been known to be a hobby for the older population as a past time. It is now considered an activity that can provide stress management for its participants across all ages. Gardening helps to improve physical and mental health for those who practice it regularly. Through this, individuals are able to express themselves as they interact with their environment by getting out in nature and physically moving around. This allows people to re-connect with themselves and their environment. In gardening, people are able to build a network of new relationships and strengthen the preexisting ones. Communication between family members, neighbors and others can increase, allowing them to build and grow their social connections. It can also help in the process of healing and dealing with any grief or loss a person may be experiencing. This is because this activity allows people to get out into nature and spend time and connect with that environment, which can feel healing and therapeutic in itself.

Gardening has health benefits much like as a therapeutic exercise. It can be a form of meditation that allows the gardener to shed daily stressors and experience peace in their moment-to-moment existence. In every aspect of gardening, whether it's planning and organizing the garden bed or planting seeds or pulling weeds, it requires focus and attention to detail. With this focus in the moment, someone is able to escape the hustle and bustle of life.

If you want to be successful in helping someone else, the first step is to understand and build a relationship with them. This can be related to what good gardening does for us. It gives us time to build a connection with nature and ourselves that promotes health and well-being. Growing your own food, feeding yourself and those you love, and having a space of your own allows you to have control over what you eat and what healthy lifestyle you want. Gardening can be done at any level from being a novice to an expert. As long as you, the gardener wants to consistently plant something in your garden, you will be successful in your pursuit of self-sufficiency. This is because gardening improves self-sufficiency for you as the individual, your family, and your community.

If you live in the city and have a small balcony, deck, driveway or other bit of outdoor space you would like to fill with plants then an urban garden is for you. If so, it is important to consider what type of plants will thrive in your area and get the most benefit from your time and attention.Most urban gardens are created from beds and as there are many other types of plant containers, planting on beds have been the most popular type.

Gardening is a sustainable form of agriculture that uses little land space to produce fresh vegetables and fruits in various communities throughout the world. It is also often practiced as a hobby or lifestyle decision by individuals in cities and suburban areas. There is also this newer concept in gardening called Urban gardening where growers typically plant vegetables or herbs in containers that can be placed on a balcony, porch, or rooftop, given that more and more people live in urban areas and cities in big concrete buildings. Raised beds can be placed in an urban setting by using old tires, wooden boxes, metal sheets, bricks or cement blocks. There are different methods to build a raised garden bed and depending on the available materials in your area you may have to improvise.

Urban gardening is often seasonal, but there are year-round options that can ensure you're producing and making the most of your gardens year round. In temperate and arid areas urban gardeners can grow a wide variety of vegetables throughout the year by using greenhouses to extend the season. Indoor gardening is also another concept that can be used and has the same ideas as greenhouse gardening, using LED lights for growing.

When you choose urban gardening as your interest, you need to know the right plants that grow well in the conditions of your region. You also need to learn the best methods for maintaining healthy plants once they are planted.

Gardening is the practice and act of growing plants or crops in a garden. It includes work tasks such as soil preparation, planting, weeding, and other general maintenance. It can range from a hobby, to an occupation, to a lifestyle. Gardening incorporates landscaping and horticulture as well as other art forms. It's not just about flowers in gardens either but also about vegetable plots, fruit trees and sustainable landscapes as well.

Gardening is one way to take care of the environment and one's family. It's also about spending time in the outdoors with friends and family. This activity also provides opportunities for people to grow their own food, participate in the community, learn about plants, and discover new ways to use plants as part of daily life. While gardening is a way for people to work together toward common goals, it can also be enjoyed alone in solitude or even with friends and family.

Since the dawn of time, people have planted seeds to help them survive and feed their families. Over time, gardening has developed and grown into a craft involving sophisticated tools and techniques. Gardening is now a science where proper planting, fertilizing and watering techniques can regulate plant growth. These techniques also help to control pests, improve yields and create healthy plant varieties.

The modern garden provides an opportunity for people to express themselves through the variety of plants and gardens they create. People are always looking for new strategies to make their gardens unique and fun.

Gardening is not just for hobbyists and gardeners. With the environmental threats people face today, it's more important than ever to grow food, maintain a healthy lifestyle, and practice sustainable practices.

Gardening can give children a chance to learn skills that can benefit them for the rest of their lives. It also provides opportunities for families to get outside and spend more time together. This is no doubt a good way to start a lifelong hobby or passion.

There are many different types of gardening methods, and it varies between vast different mediums, and also whether it's indoor or outdoor. It's also a good way to spend time with family and friends. Gardening is also about growing healthy food and enjoying the fruits of your labor, therefore giving you fulfilment!

Gardening today is as much about leaving a legacy as it is about producing food for the table or flowers for the vase. People are searching for new ways to use plants in their communities and in the environment. Dealing with such issues as global warming, sustainability, overcrowding and global agriculture will require many different approaches to gardening. This also in my opinion, the micro way to help address food shortage, and if it becomes global, then imagine the massive impact that will have to help Mother Nature.

Gardening is not limited to any geographical region or climate zone. This practice can take place within a traditional greenhouse, be it heated or not. It can also take place within greenhouses that are portable or sectionalized for each purpose. It can take place in a raised bed garden, container gardens, or in a garden plot.

Gardening is not only limited to plants either. It can also involve growing food for livestock, aquaculture and bees. Gardening can be practiced indoors using hydroponics and aeroponics as well as outdoors using traditional soil and natural elements to grow the plants without the use of synthetic chemicals to do so.

Gardening may also be a form of therapy. It can be relaxing, even therapeutic. When one is getting stressed out they can go to the garden and usually feel better because they are getting their hands dirty and being productive in nature. Gardening is a way to get in touch with nature and have fun while doing it too!

History of Gardening

The history of gardening could be traced back several thousand years ago, when people began to cultivate crops and plants in order to ensure their survival.

Gardening may be as old as humankind. A living garden, managed for its aesthetic and recreational value, was found at the Palace of King Ashurbanipal in Nineveh from about 650 BC.

The word "garden" derives from the Latin word "hortus" or "orticum", which refers to the enclosed area of a Roman villa that was planted with flowers, fruit trees, herbs and vegetables. Roman gardens were influenced by Hellenistic, Persian gardens and Asian gardens such as the Chinese tradition of Taoism. Gardens were traditionally made with herbs for medicinal use, and they also served the purpose to show off wealth and social position. Wealthy Roman citizens would grow gardens within the compounds of their villas.

Medieval European monasteries (and later the church) used herb gardens extensively for medicinal purposes and often included garden houses. These were enclosed areas where medical plants or herbs were grown. The use of garden beds and herb gardens is a form of traditional herbalism.

Horticulture, like agriculture but different in many ways, developed in ancient Egypt and lasted until about the 7th century BCE until it was replaced by less formal horticulture in Syria. There is evidence of Mesopotamian horticulture. The Greek historian Herodotus mentions the Gardens of Babylon, which were laid out by order of their first monarch, King Nimrod.

Gardening became popular in Europe in the middle Ages, and was rediscovered by Europeans during the Renaissance (14th century). The ancient Greeks and Romans had garden complexes outside their city walls, including the gardens created at Heliopolis. These garden beds contained herbs and other crops, used for food or medicinal purposes. Roman agro-culture flourished in the Imperial gardens of Constantinople.

Since the Renaissance, the creation of gardens has been more or less based on formal designs and enclosed paths. In horticulture, a garden can be defined as a visual display of plants, laid out on beds that are often mown and edged with shrubs and trees. However, in ecology, "garden" is also used to describe a more general area in which plants grow and mature for environmental reasons or where they form a mature ecosystem. In this sense, a garden is more or less synonymous with its traditional meaning of an enclosed area for raising plants.

History of gardens in the United States

The Colonial period in America was a time of European exploration and colonization. In the early years, settlers were interested only in establishing their colonies and producing necessary commodities such as food and clothing. However, by 1700, Americans began to develop gardens for aesthetic purposes. At this time they began to value their American-grown flowers, fruits, and vegetables. The growing desire for natural landscapes led to the creation of the first American gardens.

English settlers brought garden design with them, which was greatly influenced by their knowledge of English 16th-century gardens. Colonial gardens were restrained, formal and symmetrical in design, with grassy lawns and shaded by trees planted in linear patterns. Scottish settlers added many asymmetrical elements, with features such as large gardens surrounded by high walls, called "high dykes"; these are found along the North American coast from Massachusetts to Virginia.

The gardens of Charleston, South Carolina, helped establish the colonial trend for high raised beds of flowers and vegetables. The 18th century saw the development of large English-style gardens in the middle colonies during the time of George Washington. By 1800, American gardens began to reflect the intense Romantic feelings about nature among Americans in general. The design styles were influenced by European writings on garden design and gardening lore

As America became more populated after 1820, gardens became more formal. The middle and southern states featured formal plantings and ornamentation. The north and west of the country were more active in their use of landscaping to create gardens, particularly for urban areas.

Gardening Tools And Their Uses

The majority of gardening tools are made from metal. Metal tools come in a variety of shapes and sizes. Shapes of metal tools generally include the following: wire-cutters, scythe, spade, hoe and axe. Gardeners can choose between wood and steel garden tools as a matter of personal preference or ease of access to source materials.

Gardening tools are used for a number of different reasons. They can be used to remove weeds, to break up the soil, and to harvest the plants. The tools used in gardening can be simple or complex, depending upon the needs of the gardener and type of garden being tended. They must also be sturdy enough to withstand tough use and last for many years.

1A

A spade (see image 1A) is a digging instrument with a long handle attached perpendicular to a short, flat blade. Garden spades are used for digging holes and breaking up the soil. One side of the blade is serrated, allowing it to cut through the soil more easily. However, this lets weeds penetrate the blade easier, so they must be removed frequently to prevent them from growing back in.

1B

A hoe (see image 1B) is a flat-bladed tool with a long handle attached to one end of a sturdy metal shaft with some having a small pointed tip on the other end.

1C

A Shovel (see image 1C) is a long-handled tool with a flat edge used for digging. It is similar to a spade, but its wide handle holds more soil than the blade of a spade and therefore allows the gardener greater leverage in loosening the soil.

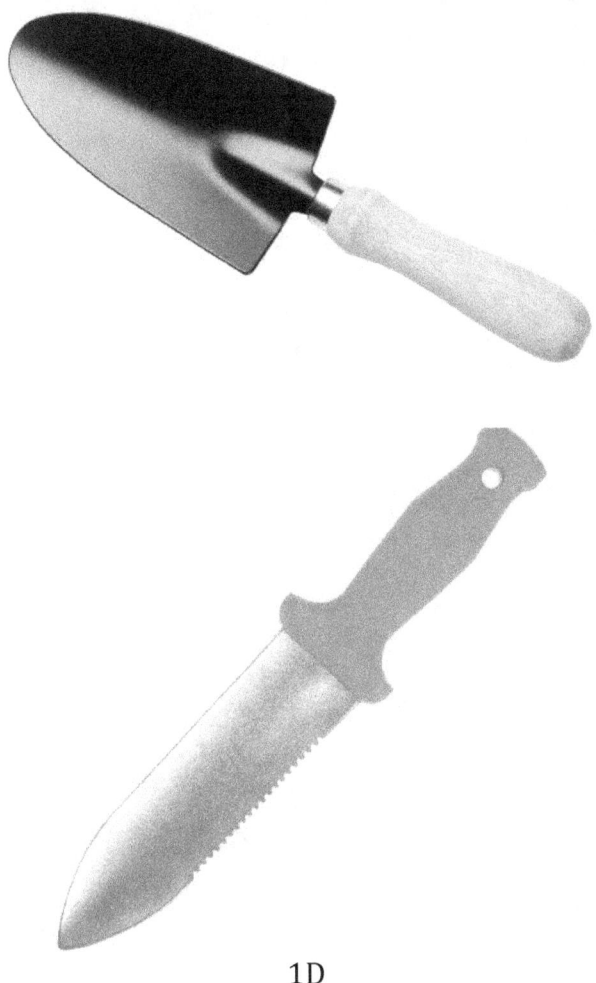

1D

A light gage garden rake (see image 1D) has short tines and may have rows of teeth along its length to help loosen clods.

1E

A trowel (see image 1E) is a flat-bladed digging tool with a moderately long handle attached to the end of a short, sturdy metal shaft. It has a wide blade on one side and is used for breaking up the ground at the root of plants. Furthermore, it is useful when transplanting seedlings or bulbs into their own dirt pots.

1F

A soil knife (see image 1F) uses a short metal blade attached to a long wooden handle to slice into and remove weeds from soil directly.

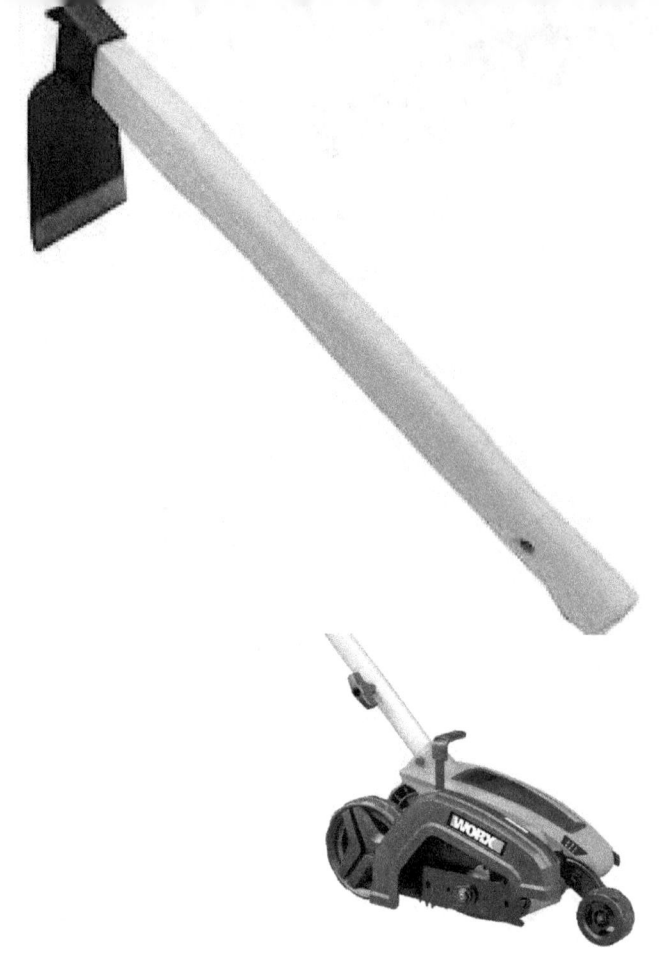

1F

An edger (see image 1F) is used for shaping beds and borders and creating borders around grass. It is also used for cutting the lawn or sods in seams (mulching). Edgers are available with flat, straight blades or with S-shaped blades that curve outward.

1G

A lawn rake (see image 1G) is a small hand-rake.

1H

A mower (see image 1H) is a small tool for cutting grass, also called a transverse mower.

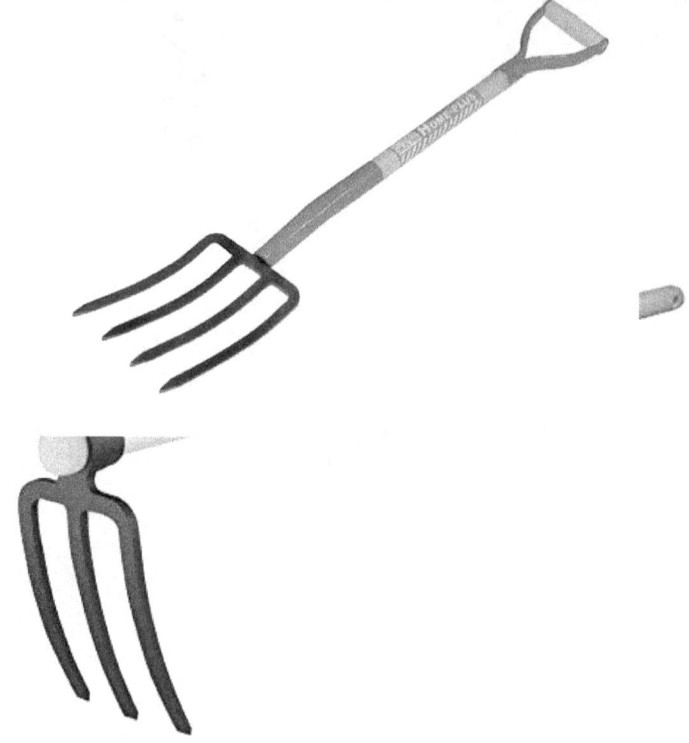

1I

A spading fork (see image 1I) is a long-handled fork used for digging holes. It consists of a slender tine attached to the end of a short stick. Gardeners can adjust the rake to fit their needs by changing the angle at which it rests on the ground as they dig.

1J

A hoe fork (see image 1J) consists of two separate tools: a hoe and an inverted fork. One end of the handle has a blade with a straight, sharpened edge and the other has a curved, bladed tine. The hoe fork can be used for digging up weeds, cultivating soil, and loosening soil near roots.

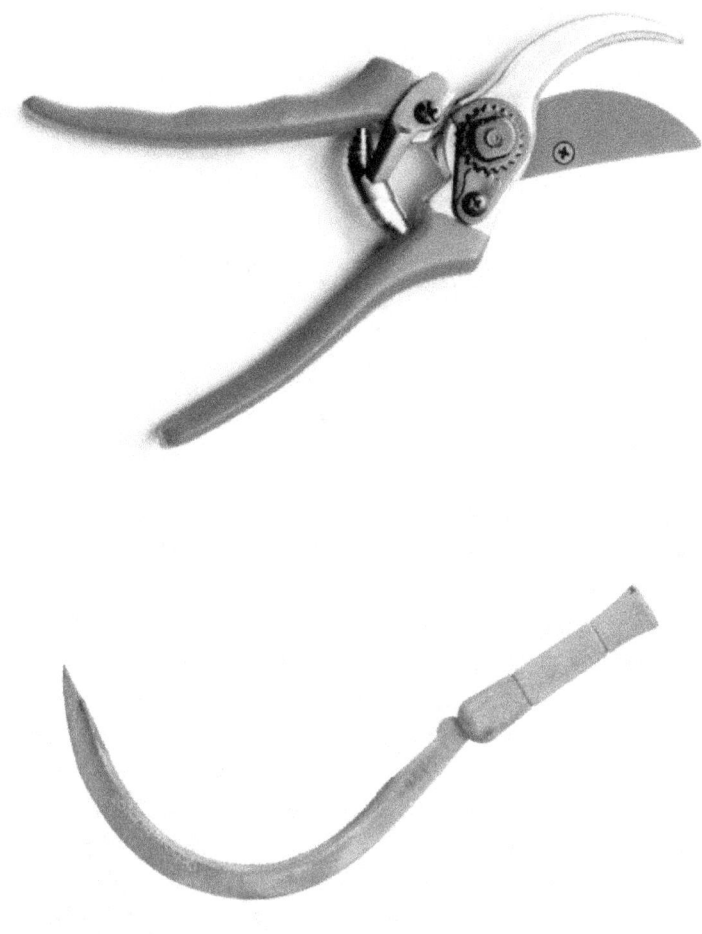

1K

Pruning shears (see image 1J) have pointed blades used for pruning. Shears can be a handheld or table-mounted tool. When the tool is held with the handles facing outward, it is called a hand shear. It can be single or double-bladed and has small handles that allow for a greater amount of precision during use. A table-mounted pruner is commonly called a tripod pruner because of its three legs supporting one central point of the pruner. This consists of a blade that is attached to a handle with handles facing in opposite directions. When the tool is held with the blades facing outward, it is called a double- or triple-bladed pruner and has sharp blades that can be used for cutting shoots.

1L

A hand scythe (see image 1L) is used to remove dead, damaged or diseased grass from lawns. It consists of a curved metal and has a small handle.

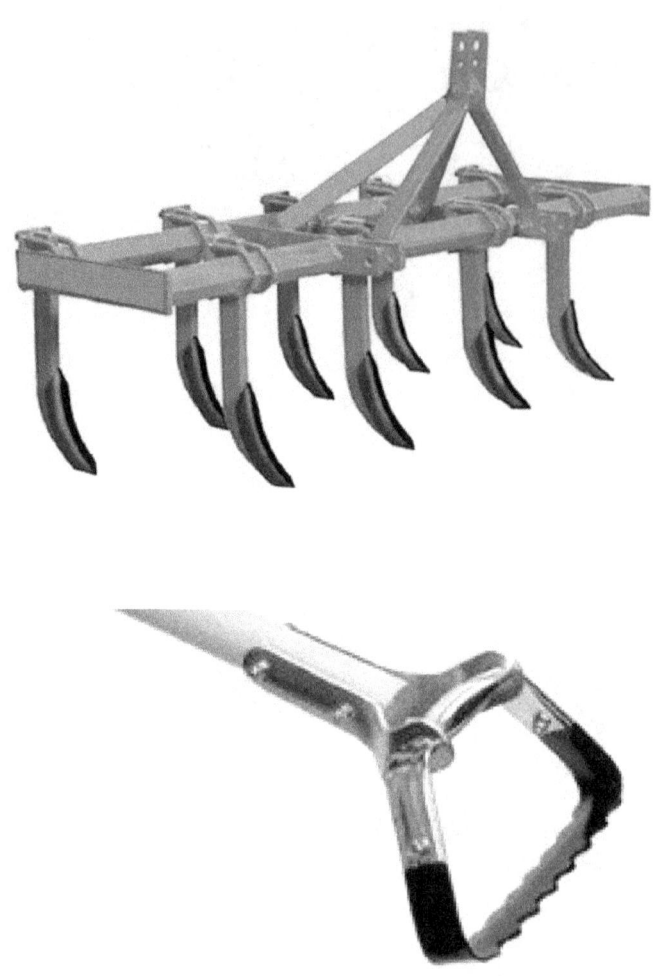

1M

A cultivator (see image 1M) has metal prongs designed to tear through soil without digging it up while also loosening it. The tool is pulled back and forth as an operator walks along the rows in which plants are growing. The tool is often connected to a long handle that allows the operator to walk through rows of plants and remove weeds without damaging them.

1N

A scuffle hoe (see image 1N) is a tool that allows operators to move horizontally or vertically through the soil. The tool consists of a long metal blade held in place by two handles. It is commonly used to loosen soil before planting or to remove plants that have been grown too deeply in the ground.

10

A stake is a rod (see image 1O) with a hook on the end used to lay posts in the ground. Stakes are typically made of metal.

1P

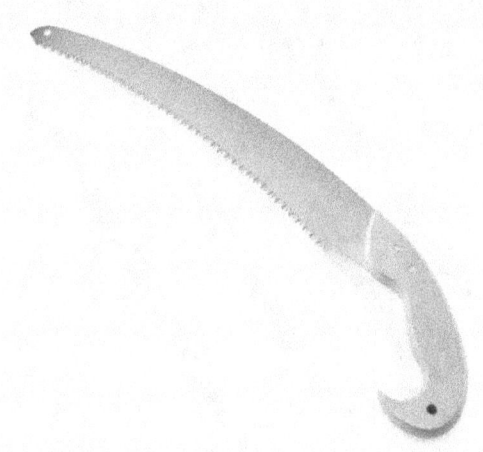

A wheelbarrow (see image 1P) is used to move items around the garden. It moves by rolling along the ground in front of the operator. The operator must push, pull, or lift to guide the wheelbarrow through open space above the ground, such as gardens or a lawn, in which it is used. A garden cart also works for moving plants and other objects around parks and at home. Garden carts usually have a small basket attached to one side. Garden carts are often used to move plants and other objects around in the garden, but they can also be used as wheelbarrows when needed.

1Q

A pruning saw see image 1Q) is a hand tool used to cut through limbs and small branches. It consists of a long blade with a handle on either side. Pruning saws are typically short and curved slightly backward, with the larger teeth toward the blade's tip. Like other saws, pruning saws are able to cut by moving the two opposite handles in opposite directions while applying pressure between them to force the blade against an object.

1R

A garden scissor (see image 1R) is a hand tool used for cutting and separating materials. The scissors consists of a straight, sturdy blade paired with a more flexible blade. To cut material with the straight blade, the operator moves the stiff blade across the object while pushing down in the middle. To cut sections apart, separate them with their thumb and forefinger while pulling back on both handles. Scissors are not to be confused with other hand tools called shears, which typically consist of a wide blade and two handles, or snips, which typically consist of two straight blades with their handles attached on a hinge.

1S

A broom (see image 1S) is hand tool used for sweeping floors, collecting dirt, and cleaning walls. Brooms typically have a small handle at the top where the user pushes down to sweep or pull up to collect dirt. Brooms come in various shapes and sizes; some have long handles while others have short handles.

Types of Home Gardens

You could create a beautiful and welcoming space in your own yard by adding a garden. Adding a garden to your property may seem like a daunting task, but it is actually easy and you'll love it once you get the hang of it! You can find many different types of gardens that are perfect for any size or shape of property.

Small Gardens:

If you are living in apartment or have limited outdoor space available, you can still enjoy the benefits of gardening on a patio, balcony, deck or porch. Growing plants in containers allow you to make the most of any small space.

Terracing:

Terrace gardens are an excellent way to create a beautiful outdoor space, even on a limited parcel of land. With terracing, you can take advantage of every inch of your land and grow fruit trees, flowering perennials and other plants with little or no maintenance. The key to this type of garden is planning for what will be planted so you make the most out of your narrow space.

Infill Gardens:

Infill gardens typically add a few feet of garden space to a small yard, and can offer several benefits to your yard. Because infill gardens are usually located in tight spaces, plants can grow vertically, taking up less space horizontally. It is also a brilliant method to add privacy between properties as it closes up any potential view through the fence and shrubs in the garden.

Rain Gardens:

Rain gardens are great for yards with poor soil or areas that receive water during heavy storms. In a rain garden, the water is collected and stored for use by plants and other living things that are able to survive on the rain from nature, rather than needing to be watered by hand. A rain garden typically looks like a bog or marsh area, and is typically planted with native plants that thrive in wet conditions. This type of garden helps keep your yard green all year long, even during times of drought.

Focal Gardens:

Focal gardens are a great way to add a focal point to your yard and add interest and beauty. The focal garden can be on a small corner of your property, or even exist as part of the landscape surrounding the house. Focal gardens often feature plants that create a color or theme of a certain color throughout the entire garden. This type of garden works well in smaller yards, and can be finished in a few short weeks.

Kitchen Gardens:

A kitchen garden is a great way to add vegetables and herbs to your home in a small space. Kitchen gardens are typically located indoors in large, open kitchens, and are perfect for growing small amounts of produce. Kitchen gardens feature items that are easy to grow including perennial herbs like basil, parsley, chives and mint, which can be used throughout the course of a year.

Bonsai:

Bonsai gardens are great for adding miniature trees or shrubs to your yard. You can create your own miniature evergreen trees or plant a number of different flowering bonsai bushes in an outdoor planter to add interest and color to a small area. Bonsai are usually pruned on a regular basis to keep them small, and bonsai gardens are an excellent way to add beauty anywhere.

Herb Gardens:

Herb gardens are a very good way to add an organic feel to your home, and they add beauty and taste to your favorite dishes. You can create an herb garden on any scale by adding herbs to containers or planting them in the ground. Herbs are usually planted in containers, and they are easy to care for. Herbs make great indoor plants, but they can also be grown outdoors with little or no maintenance.

Fruit & Nut Gardens:

Fruit gardens are an excellent way to make use of any available space. You can create a fruit garden in containers, and even plant trees in your yard. Fruit plants are very easy to care for, and they attract wildlife. It is easy to grow some of your favorite fruit or nut trees in an outdoor garden, and many fruit-bearing plants can be grown outdoors if you know what you're doing.

Perennial Gardens:

Perennial gardens are a great way to establish a beautiful and lush area in your yard without having to prune or transplant every year. Perennial gardens can be planted in any type of soil, and require little or no pruning, so you can create a garden with no maintenance responsibilities. When growing perennials, you must enjoy the benefits of living with perennial plants for many years.

Cafe Gardens:

Cafe gardens are beautiful framed areas that make it look like everything is growing within the planters. You can create a cafe garden by using small planters on an arbor or deck. Cafe gardens typically feature plants that are easy to maintain, and are a beautiful addition to any outdoor area.

Water Gardens:

Water gardens are an excellent way to add beauty and color to your yard. Water gardens require little maintenance, and there is minimal work involved when you want to create a water garden. Water gardens are especially great for adding color, and they can easily be part of your outdoor planter.

Paver Gardens:

Paver gardens are beautiful, mosaic-like areas that make it look like the area was once a garden. You can create a paver garden by placing pavers in the lawn, creating smaller areas of paving around trees or other objects. Paver gardens look great year round as they create an even-colored landscape all year long.

Orchard Garden

Orchard gardening is another form of gardening with more potential yields than simple fruit growing. It involves an entire orchard or a part of one, which can be planted with the same variety of fruit. For example, an apple orchard requires planting the same variety of apples. Some orchards are so large that they require multiple varieties for optimal yields and taste. Others have multiple uses for their products, such as cider production. Orchards need skilled gardeners to maintain this type of gardening, including pruning trees to prevent disease, help in pollination, and take care of pest issues.

Other Types Of Gardening

The simplest type of gardening is **fruit growing**. It entails planting and tending a given plant, and harvesting the fruit when it ripens. Some gardeners are interested in growing the perfect fruit, rather than producing large amounts. This type of gardening often involves knowledge of tree pruning techniques to reduce disease and increase sunlight exposure on fruits, as well as advanced training in grafting and cloning techniques to get superior fruit varieties.

Perennial gardening is simply the growing of perennial plants. It is a type of ornamental gardening, involving the use of well-established plants that live for multiple years that are not grown annually from seed. Perennial gardens are long-term investments; many people, such as botanist F.A. Bazzaz, consider them to be more important to the ecology because their existence promotes biodiversity and wildlife habitats and provides breeding areas for birds and pollinators.

Hydroponics is a subset of hydroculture, where the solid medium that plants grow in is either composed of mineral salts or water. Hydroponic gardening is a type of hydroculture and therefore subject to the same conditions of hydroculture: The medium must be fertile, it must be able to retain water without becoming waterlogged, and must be able to drain excess water. Hydroponic gardening is most often used in areas with an absence or scarcity of soil.

Aeroponics is a type of hydroponics that involves growing plants in an air or mist environment, rather than in soil. While this can be done with any type of plant, it is most commonly used on herbaceous or leafy vegetables.

Aquaponics is a kind of hydroponics that involves growing plants in water. The water provides nutrients to the plants through bacteria, which are grown in tanks and fed waste from the fish tanks below them. Fish are kept in the tank for waste removal; water from their tank is pumped up to the plant tanks via pipes, where it provides nutrients to the plants.

Groundcovers are plants that grow over and below the soil for protection or camouflage (hence "ground"). They make up a majority of the overall green area in lawns. Because they are not rooted in the soil, groundcovers do not share the same nutritional requirements as other plants, and therefore need to be fed specific nutrients. When a can of fertilizer is put next to a plant, it will absorb the nutrients on the outer surface of the leaf. Many groundcovers are grown for their ornamental value, such as ivy and other plants that cover walls. Others grow well even if they are not beautiful, such as corn stalks, which need to be kept strong and healthy to prevent them from being bent or torn from the ground by wind or frost.

Urban Farming Techniques

Raised bed farming

2a

Raised bed farming (see image 2A) is an approach that can be used to help make food production more efficient. In addition to being space efficient, raised bed farming also allows for the collection of all the runoff from gardening activities. This runoff could be used as a nutrient-rich liquid fertilizer for the food plants. The planting beds could also be placed over a layer of soil which would act as a protection from the rain that would naturally fall onto the garden. Raised bed farming makes it easy to maintain the beds and place plants in them. It also makes it easier to harvest food. In this method, the beds are basically built on top of the existing earth. This gives one the ability to use more land for agricultural purposes and allows one to maximize crop yields because they do not have to rotate crops too often.

Raised bed gardening can also help save money on minerals and soil amendments such as peat moss because it allows for good drainage and aeration.

Vegetable garden

2B

A vegetable garden (see image 2B) is a garden that produces vegetables and herbs for human and animal nutrition. It can be like a small individual container of tomatoes or as big as a full acre garden. Vegetables come in a variety of types such as leafy and root vegetables. Some are grown for the seeds, others for the leaves and some can be eaten both ways. The weather conditions, soil quality and location affect what is grown. Vegetables are the most important food supply within a garden, because they provide the largest portion of nutrition from the garden to humans. Various sites have different conditions that are suited to growing specific vegetables, which can help with production yields from your garden.
A vegetable garden can be particularly effective if it is used as part of a food forest. This is beneficial to the gardeners because they do not have to walk very far in order to harvest their produce. Also, it is a closed-system which reduces the amount of water needed to grow plants in the garden. To achieve this, you need to place some kind of barrier around the garden such as stone or wooden fences. Another way you can create a natural barrier is by planting trees around the vegetable garden.

Microgreen Farming

2C

Microgreen farms (see image 2C) are small farms usually no more than one acre large. They are almost always specialized in just one crop and use high-yield farming techniques. In addition, microgreen farms never harvest more than they need but keep a buffer stock of seeds for replanting.

Microgreen greenhouses have the advantage that they can be as small as five by nine meters while still providing enough space to grow Microgreens and other crops. The term microgreen is used because these greens used are very young versions of their full grown counterparts. When growing vegetables, micro-farmers use a wide variety of methods to increase crop yields. These include mechanical cultivation, hydroponic production, organic farming, and permaculture.

Vertical gardening

(See image 2D)

2D

This technique uses towers to increase the amount of production or cut down on costs. Towers can be constructed out of old shipping containers, water barrels and wooden pallets. In addition to the cost savings vertical gardening also conserves space and can be done either indoors or outdoors like in soil or hydroponically.

Positioning of crops is important because it reduces shade onto other plants and allows for more sunlight and water. Vertical gardens are sometimes organized in rows, allowing for easy access in addition to saving space.

Square foot garden

2E

Square foot garden (see image 2E) is a method of gardening that is used in small plots or areas. This method uses rows of crops which are arranged in a grid pattern. In addition this method requires the gardener to use raised beds because it increases the growing area and efficiency of the garden significantly. The square foot garden will use a mixture of intensive and extensive growing methods. The intensive growing methods primarily use raised beds in which the grower fills the bed with a material that is stacked one on top of the next. The intensive growing methods will be chemical free, water efficient and full spectrum. The extensive growing methods will use only organic methods such as compost and decomposed manure.

Container garden

2F

A container garden (see image 2F) is an outdoor garden that uses containers as its main growing media. In addition to the plastic containers used for the soil they also use other types of containers like tubs and baskets. The main purpose of a container garden is to reduce the amount of work and materials required to produce large amounts of food. Container gardening is used for both intensive and extensive types of planting. The benefits of container gardening are the reduction in labor, materials and expenses. Another benefit of container gardening is that it can be used in almost any climate or area, indoor or outdoor. Containers can be made out of metal, plastic and glass.

No Dig Garden

(see image 2G)

2G

These gardens rely on mulches and cover crops rather than digging. In the no dig garden, tillage is used to control weeds and grasses, but not to prepare a seed bed. Mulches are simply a layer of non-decomposing material that is laid over the soil surface or added as a mix into the top layer of soil for plants to grow through. Cover crops are grown primarily for their ability to provide organic matter and nutrients rather than their ability to be harvested as a crop.

The advantages of a no-dig garden are that it provides a more natural growing environment for plants and reduces the amount of work required to maintain the garden. The disadvantages are that it takes more time than other methods and it requires more maintenance.

Types of Floral Gardens

There are several types of gardens that can be found in parks. Most of the themes for these gardens are quite specific. The most common in city parks tends to be the rose garden, the seasonal flower garden, the herb garden, and the butterfly garden. However, there are many other types that can be found in public and private places, such as:

Bird Habitat – This type of garden is designed to attract birds by offering food sources and water for them to drink from. Bird gardens are often located near water to attract birds.

Hawthorn – These shrubs have thorny branches and are usually found in the windy areas of parks. Their thorns help to deter rodents such as rabbits and deer. They also provide a valuable source of food for birds and other small animals.

Mushrooms – These are known as "fairy rings" because they look like a magical circle made from soil after a rain. Many different varieties of mushrooms can be found in these circles.

Rose – These are often planted in parks because of their beauty and the relaxing effect that they have. Rose gardens are great for those who want to enjoy a tranquil setting right outside their doorstep.

Shade Garden – These gardens contain plants that thrive in shady areas. They can be found near trees, buildings, or other large structures that provide shade for the garden area.

Labyrinth Style - The type of garden that is like a maze can be enjoyed by children, as well as adults. One might even consider placing a maze in their garden to help reduce the time spent looking for lost items. One type of maze that can be found in nature parks is called the butterfly garden. This type of garden is quite detailed with benches, paths, walkways, and even fish ponds to attract butterflies.

Garden for Kids – Children can usually enjoy the types of gardens that feature animals or other creatures, such as the zoo or aquarium garden. These types of gardens generally have pathways that wind through a nature-like setting, where the animals or creatures can be near visitors.

When choosing the type of garden for your home, the first key is to be aware of the climate and other conditions in your area. For example, if you live in a dry, hot area and want to grow a garden that relies mainly on rainfall rather than irrigation, choose plants which require less water and shade such as succulents.

Next, consider the type of soil and other conditions in your garden. If you have a very well-drained soil that is rich in nutrients, you can plant herb plants on the sunny side of your path or border. However, if your garden contains both sandy soil and poor nutrients then you must start with planting some young and nutritious plants such as native plants which can be grown from seed or cuttings along the sunny side of the path or border. These will provide vital food for other less successful plants.

Finally, don't forget to consider the time of year when you are planning your garden. Plants that require a lot of maintenance will need more frequent watering during dry summer months whereas plants which are dried out less frequently will require more frequent watering during autumn and winter.

Starting A Garden

If you've been looking for a new project to take on this summer, planting a garden is the most satisfying and rewarding. It's easier than you might think. All you need is a little space – whether that's an empty lot in your neighborhood, vacant corner of your office building, or unused patch of lawn at home – and the willingness to get dirt under your nails (or soil in your hair).

The most significant step to consider when getting started in the garden is choosing a site. Add to that your own desire for a certain kind of plant – whether its flowers, vegetables, herbs or fruit - and you're well on your way to a success story.

If you still have space in your yard, or you're willing to make some more room, planting a garden is the perfect way to save money on groceries and get plenty of fresh produce. When you want your plants to grow well, however, it's not just about adding dirt. Here are a few tricks for getting the most out of your vegetable gardening efforts.

Prepare the site:

Digging 5 feet of soil is a good start, but consider adding some compost or manure to improve your soil. Compost will add the necessary nutrients to the soil and increase its water-holding capacity, while manure will help improve the composition of the soil. Don't stir up a lot of earth with a tiller or rototiller before planting; wait until after. Green manures are plants that grow quickly and then are tilled into the soil to improve it, like rye.

Sow your seeds:

Be realistic about the type of plants you're growing in your garden (pumpkins vs. lettuce; bush beans vs. pole beans). In general, smaller seeds should be planted closer together than larger ones (but always check the seed packet). If you have a small yard, plant lots of small plants instead of fewer big ones. If space is at a premium, consider filling containers with potting soil and growing plants in them until the weather warms up again.

Water your garden:

Moisten the soil before you plant each seed or seedling. This will help it to absorb water and nutrients. Bigger seeds like carrots or corn should be planted deeper than smaller ones, so they have room to grow. You may dig a hole in the soil, remove the soil from around the seed, and drop it in. Fill in around your plants with some of the soil you removed from the hole. After planting, water your garden every day for two weeks.

Plant flowers:

Smaller plants can have large flowers, like peas and snapdragons. With time, you'll see all kinds of flowers blooming from your garden. Lilacs, for example, are a great addition to your yard. The flowers bloom in the spring and last all summer long.

Plant herbs:

You can use herbs in everything from salads to bread. Parsley, basil, oregano and thyme all do well in the garden. You can even grow them indoors in window boxes or planters, especially if there's an early frost.

Plant small vegetables:

Try planting some of your garden's smallest plants, like lettuce and radishes. Radishes taste great fresh in salads, and a single plant will last you all summer long. Lettuce is also good to put in sandwiches. You can find seeds or rootstock at a nursery.

How to Prepare an Indoor Garden

One of the easiest ways to have a garden year-round is by gardening indoors. It's not difficult at all, and can be very rewarding. All you need are few common household items as well as seeds or plants. Here are some tips to help you be successful at gardening indoors.

Hydroponic Garden

4A

The days of getting a nice big plot in your backyard to grow your own vegetables are quickly coming to an end. The amount of land available for gardening is shrinking dramatically with the growth of urban sprawl, and access to fresh produce is declining due to environmental degradation. We need a new approach for growing our food that will allow us all to have gardens at home. Hydroponics is the solution.

Hydroponics (see image 4A) is an integrated system of growing that uses artificial environments and controlled irrigation to plant, grow, heal and dry plants without soil or sunlight. Hydroponics has revolutionized the way we grow food year-round because it provides a new set of options for which to grow in a balanced diet.

Hydroponics can provide unique flavor combinations for many vegetables, herbs and fruits. For example, sweet peppers, tomatoes, cucumbers and melons can be grown using the same process but in different configurations. Each method provides an alternative to traditional techniques. Hydroponics does not just provide growing space in your home; it provides a new array of growing solutions that are accessible to all types of veggie gardeners.

How to prepare:

The great thing about the hydroponic garden is that it does not require a lot of space. A small area in your home can be set aside for a healthy indoor vegetable garden. Hydroponics allows you to grow healthy vegetables and herbs with minimal effort and maximum results.

What you'll need:

<u>A mini greenhouse</u> - one that fits on a table, shelf or counter top is best. You can choose a type that can be pumped with air and water. A soil-free growing medium such as perlite or lava rock made of volcanic rock works best but a mix of sand and vermiculite also works well. These are lightweight materials, so you can move your plants from room to room or plant them in containers for ease of storage. Systems that use water and air pumps can be placed on a small table or hung from the ceiling.

<u>Hydroponic nutrient solutions</u> - these usually come as powders or liquids and are made from organic material. These will provide your plants with the nutrients they need to grow vigorously and reach their full potential.

<u>A light source</u> - this could be as simple as a sunny window, compact fluorescent bulbs, fluorescent tubes, incandescent bulbs, or a combination of bulbs of different wattage levels.

<u>A place for the plants to be watered</u> - this needs to be close to your growing area. You can use one of several watering systems that will provide water in a steady stream.

<u>A device for measuring the water and nutrients</u> - there are many types of hydroponic nutrient systems available, but some of them are more convenient and easy to administer.

<u>Plants</u> - you should begin by planting lettuce that has a vigorous growing habit. It is essential that you choose the proper variety that will grow well in your hydroponic garden.

How to start

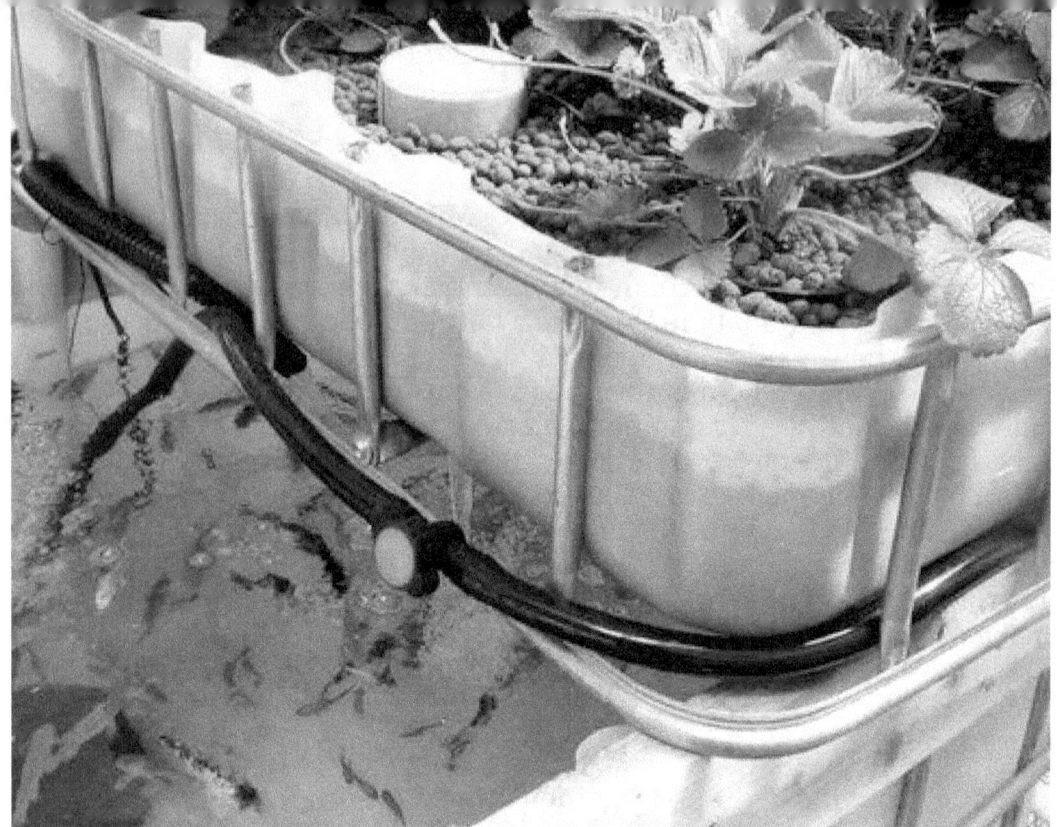

You can start by filling your mini greenhouse with all the growing media you need. This could include perlite, lava rock and a combination of sand and vermiculite. These materials should be moistened so moisture collects below the growing medium. There are variety of ways to grow plants in a hydroponic system, but it is important that you first learn how they work in order to know how much water, nutrients and air to give each plant. The ideal situation is being able to monitor everything, but since this may not be possible for you, you should learn the basics of how each plant grows.

You can use a bubbler system, wick system, ebb and flow hydroponic system or NFT (nutrient film technique) method for your garden. Each method can provide nutrients to your plants in a certain way. The more you know about them, the more effective in growing you will be.

Before planting your seeds or seedlings, you should be sure that the nutrients are available to your plants. There are variety of ways in which you can do this. They include using a top feeder, bottom feeder or a drip system.

Aquaponic garden

4B

One of the benefits of an Aquaponic garden (see image 4B) is that it's easy to set up and maintain. Read these instructions and follow them diligently for a healthy, productive garden all year round.

How to Prepare:

Step 1 - Drill 2 holes in the bottom corner of the tank, one hole at each end. Thread a piece of clear plastic tubing through each hole so that it reaches just above water level, then seal with silicone or glue to prevent leaks. Assure that the tube is not kinked or clogged.

Step 2 - Place a flat rock inside the tank to support the pump. The rock must fit snugly into the corners, but must not be wider than 1" for the tank to remain upright. A flat rock is recommended because it will reduce vibration during use, as all pumps make some noise.

Step 3 - Place a small electrical timer on the pump's output to allow for sufficient time for CO_2 generation. It is suggested that the pump be run for 20 minutes per hour.

Step 4 - Fish to your heart's content! Glassfish are very tolerant and do not require warm water. That said, it is recommended that you do not introduce them into your garden until it has been running for at least a few weeks.

Step 5 - Place the plants in their pots so they fit snugly in the tank. Be sure to position about 12" of gravel beneath them to ensure that they can sink their roots and remain upright.

Step 6 - Fill the tank to 2" less than the top with water from your garden hose or tap. A pH of 7.5 is recommended, but this can be adjusted later if necessary.

Step 7 - Plug the pump into a timer and let it run for 24 hours to establish your nitrifying bacteria colony. For the next day, keep the tank covered to ensure that the fish do not escape.

Step 8 - For optimal health and growth, a pH of 7.5 is ideal for your plants. When your pH is too high or low, you can adjust it now with aquarium chemicals ("pH Up" and "pH Down").

Step 9 - Slowly add food to your tank after at least 24 hours have passed since you filled up the tank. Begin with just a few pellets, then gradually increase the amount if your fish are not consuming them.

Step 10 - Within a few days, Nitrogen Cycle Bacteria will have established themselves in your tank to process leftover food and convert it into nitrite and ammonia. This is great news! Plants can utilize nitrate ($NO3$) as well as nitrite ($NO2$) for growth.

Step 11 - While waiting for your bacteria colony to catch up, you can add your fish. A low nitrogen diet is recommended until the bacteria have had time to establish itself. If you want to use fish, wait 6 weeks to introduce new fish into the tank. To ensure that your bacteria colony has plenty of food and that you won't make too many ammonia spikes, it is recommended that you do nothing else in the tank other than feed and care for the plants.

Step 12 - If necessary, when the pH is between 6.5 and 7.5, use a small amount of aquarium "pH Up" to adjust it.

Step 13 - Now that your bacteria colony has gotten up to speed, you can add more plants if you wish. You may also want to add ornaments and other decorations now as well. Do not feed the fish excess food or they will have ammonia spikes and die off. It's always better to feed them less than more.

Step 14 - Monitor your ammonia and nitrite levels. Nitrite will continue to rise for a few days while your bacteria colony is catching up with its food intake. After 24 hours, it should fall to an acceptable level. Aim for 3-5 ppm of nitrite in the water.

Step 15 - When you are happy with the tank's ammonia and nitrite levels, you can add fish.

Step 16 - Rinse out the pots to clean out any fertilizer or bacteria residue.

Step 17 - Plant the plants in your pots so they fit snugly into your tank. Be sure to position about 12" of gravel beneath them to ensure that they can sink their roots and remain upright.

Step 18 - Fill the tank with 2" less than the top with water from your garden hose or tap. A pH of 7.5 is recommended, but this can be adjusted later if necessary.

Aeroponic garden

4C

Aeroponics (see image 4C) is a type of growing that uses no soil. All you need are a few buckets, some water, and light to grow vegetables and herbs either indoors or in small gardens. It is an easy way to have fresh food year-round and all the time!
Aeroponics means you don't need dirt or fertilizer. And it will keep pests away because they can't get through the fine mist that is sprayed onto the plants at regular intervals. You will never need to dig up the plant or worry about keeping the soil moist.

Aeroponics uses less water than potted plants because the water comes out of a sprayer. And you will not worry about watering because the system that sprays out water is automated. But you can use your finger to spread around dust or other nutrients if you want.

How to prepare:

You are going to need two plastic pots and something to prop them up. It could be a bucket or another pot. The only rule is that the water can't sit on the bottom of the pots or there won't be any oxygen and it will ruin your plants.
And you will need some PVC pipe, a pump, tubing, light and of course seeds.
Cut holes in the bottom of both buckets and put one end of the PVC pipe into each hole. Turn it so that it is centered well.
Take the other end of the pipe and stick it into the pump. Put a net pot on top of each pot. The net pots will have holes in them to put the seeds in.
Put some water in each bucket. You don't need much or you'll make a big mess.
Put the tubing around the outside of both buckets so that they are level with one another and twist it around to hold it in place as tightly as possible so that there will be no leaks.
Put the pump into one bucket and the other end of the tubing into the other bucket.
Put a light in each bucket if you want to speed up germination.
Pressurize the system by taking a syringe or something else that will take a little bit of air at a time and squirting it into the system. Keep doing this till all air is out of it.
Put the plastic pots in place and just put some soil on them.
And now you are ready to plant.
If you got a lot of seeds, you can choose which plants to put in each bucket and space them out. You don't need to put them in a specific order though, nor do you need to water them.
Put some seeds in the net pots, and then wait till they germinate. You can use either seeds or seedlings for this process.
When those roots are long enough to reach the bottom of the bucket, you will need to change your system.
Take off your two buckets and remove the net pots that are full of plants. Replace them with new ones with fresh seeds. Then put more water in the buckets.
Use a feeding tube to add nutrients to the soil. Wait till the plants are big enough and then start watering regularly.

Vertical garden:

4D

A vertical garden (see image 4D) is a modern garden technique that uses plants to create walls of green, while saving space and money. Vertical gardens are also sometimes called living walls or green walls, but the name "vertical garden" is the most common term used.
Ideally, you would find a spot that gets at least six hours of sunlight for your vertical gardens to grow correctly. The best soil for them is a mix of sand and compost.

How to prepare:

The first step in building your vertical garden is to pick out a frame or structure that will hold the plants. This is something as simple as a wooden frame of lattice, or you can build it out of PVC or metal piping if you want it to look more modern. You can also use just about anything that can hold soil and plants, like bamboo poles or recycled materials.
Once you have your frame or structure figured out, the next step is to fill it with soil and put in your plants. If you are living in a colder weather, you can use plastic mulch to keep the ground warm for the roots. You can also add rocks or other decorations to give your vertical garden a more finished look.
The most important aspect of growing plants vertically is keeping them well watered. The soil needs moisture to stay healthy, so it must be evenly spread through the entire structure of your garden.

Container garden

4E

Container gardening (see image 4E) is a great way to make the most of a small space. Whether you live in a small apartment, have poor soil or too much shade on your property, container gardening can help you grow healthy vegetables and flowers.

How to prepare:

First select the right size containers for your desired plants. A 20-gallon container is ideal for a tomato plant. Check the soil inside your containers for any weeds and make sure it is moist but not soggy.

Select a variety that is recommended for container gardening. Choose plants that have been bred to grow well in containers.

Fill the container with potting soil.

Place your plants in the container so they will grow in the right direction. Make sure there will be enough room for them to grow once they're mature. Plant tall plants such as tomato and pepper at the back of the container so they will not shade shorter ones such as lettuce and spinach.

Water your potted plants regularly throughout the growing season. Set a water can in a small container filled with water, and place it above the plants. This will ensure that all of the roots of your plants are kept moist.

Place your containers where they get full sun. When you live in a specific area with little or no sunlight, place them on the east side of your house to be able to grow later into the evening.

Be sure to clean and maintain your containers often. Remove any old, dying or diseased leaves.

Repot your plants if necessary. If the roots have filled the container and begin to grow out of it, repot them into a bigger container using fresh potting soil.

Harvest your vegetables when they are ready. Cut away at the base of your plant with pruners or scissors.

Remove any remaining seed stalks or immature fruit before the next harvest.

Dig Garden

4F

Dig Garden (see image 4F) is a much gentler process that does not disturb the soil as much as tilling does, which is often necessary to break up compacted ground. The idea is to loosen the surface of the ground enough that water can penetrate and drain quickly, but without causing excessive soil loss or damage to plants.

How to prepare:

Prop the shovel in a hole, then place a trowel on the top of the shovel, and use it to dig out soil. Usually you want to loosen 8-12 inches down, and be sure that you are pulling the soil out from all sides of the plant. This will help loosen compacted soil and make it easier for roots to spread. If you have a shrub, prune back any branches or stems that are growing towards the center of the plant in order to encourage lateral branch growth; this will help create a bushier, fuller plant.

Tilling:

Tilling is a process that includes the loosening of soil, but it also involves breaking up larger clumps of soil into smaller particles and stirring them into the top layer of the soil. This helps to expose the largest and deepest parts of the soil to oxygen and water, improving nutrient retention. This may be done with or without chemicals or machines; tilling breaks up the soil, allowing nutrients to be released by breaking down organic matter. This creates the opportunity for oxygen to reach the roots, which helps plants to grow larger. The opposite of tilling is no-till farming.

A hand cultivator has rotating tines with a spacing that allows it to dig in shallowly and lift the upper layers of soil.

For this process to work effectively, you should first turn over the soil by hand or using a shovel, and then use a tiller. This will increase the amount of oxygen and water in the soil. Using a garden tiller often breaks up clumps of dirt; however, when done incorrectly it can cause significant damage to your plant's root system because you are moving soil from one end of the plant to the other instead of loosening it up around the roots.

How To Choose Plants and Seedlings For Your Very Own Garden

Every region has different climate preferences and seasonal variations. That's why it's best to visit nurseries in person before making any purchases online. That way, you can see how plants look in person and also get the help of a knowledgeable staff member who could answer your questions. Many nurseries and garden centers provide a list of plants suited to your location.

<u>Choose plants that fit your space</u>

<u>Garden layout</u>: Before buying any plants, you'll need to consider what kind of garden you'd like. First, decide if you want an edging garden or a bed garden.
<u>Edging</u>: Edging gardens are a great way to control plant growth up against a property line. You can choose from Japanese yew, ornamental privet, and English ivy to create that intentional privacy. Additionally, boxwood and rhododendron grow quickly to make an attractive edge.
<u>Bed Garden</u>: A bed garden is the perfect place for those plants you love to come back year after year. Consider planting plenty of flowers, perennials, and herbs so they return year after year. Also consider planting a single-stemmed shrub or annual accent plant that will add charm and color.
<u>Protective plants:</u> Some plants can be invasive—and they don't have to be! Find plants that are more difficult to invade and you'll create a garden that is well protected. For example, there are Asian pear trees that have a difficult time spreading. And, they produce delicious fruit, too!
<u>Plant size</u>: You'll also need to consider the size the plant will eventually grow to. For example, if you only have a small space to fill, choose an herbaceous perennial or succulent instead of a big shrub. The same goes for containers: choose smaller plants and containers so that you can move them around in your garden as needed.
<u>Container gardening:</u> Finally, you'll want to choose your containers wisely. When you're planting in the ground and not using containers, make sure that the plant has a long taproot. This means it will grow deep into the ground eventually and take up most of the nutrients near the topsoil.
If you have a container garden, look for plants with small taproots and shallow roots that will begin to crowd in your container. Plants like ferns, cyclamen, and hens and chicks don't grow very deep into the ground. So, they will remain a manageable size inside your container.

<u>Choose the right plants for your gardening needs.</u>

Flowers: A great way to grow some of your produce is to plant flowers that double as food! Not only do edible flowers taste great, they give your dishes a pop of color along with their other benefits. For example, nasturtiums are edible and are a great addition to salads.

Vegetables: Vegetables are a must in any garden! They don't all require full sun, so choose your plants wisely. If you're in the North with less sunlight, look for vegetable varieties that grow well in shady areas. And, if you're in the South with more sunlight, try some of the more heat-tolerant varieties.

Herbs: Herbs are delicious and are a welcome addition to almost any meal. They can add some flair to salads and are even possible to use as a cooking spice. Herbs like basil, mint, and parsley will grow well in any garden because they don't need full sun.

Fabrics: Although it's not considered a vegetable, hemp has become an increasingly popular addition to the garden in recent years. It is an extremely sustainable plant that very easily grows with minimal upkeep during the growing season. Hemp is a great addition to any garden as it helps to filter the water and filter the air.

Perennials: Perennial plants are great because they come back year after year. Many perennial plants like bougainvillea, cosmos, and zinnias will grow quickly, adding color periodically in your garden. When you don't want to spend so much time weeding and maintaining your perennial plants, choose compact varieties that are easy to prune.

Plant Zones: Don't forget to consider the hardiness zone of the plant. Because plants react poorly to extreme temperature changes, they can be killed by incorrect planting date. For instance, a plant that thrives in zones 4-9 can be killed by planting it in zone 3. Why?

Zone 3 has an average minimum temperature of -30 to 0°F (-34 – -18 °C), while zone 4 has an average minimum temperature of -10 to 10 °F (-23 – -12 °C). The colder the condition, the longer it will take to thaw out, and the longer it takes to melt snow and ice. The plant will die due to the extreme cold before it can thaw out and recover.

Be sure to research your hardiness zones to guide you in deciding when and what to plant. Resources are available about global and local hardiness zones.

Mulch: If you're planting a vegetable garden, mulch is a great way to keep all your plants healthy. Mulch is an organic material that could be added to the garden to help control moisture and weeds.

Good soil: Before you choose any plants, make sure you have good garden soil already in place. Plants need nitrogen, phosphorus, potassium and micronutrients to grow so make sure your soil has enough nutrients for your plants. Then, you can add a few key amendments to get the most out of your garden.

Sometimes the most beautiful plants are those you have to do little maintenance with. However, if you're looking for the biggest tomato, choose one that needs lots of water and is seasonal. If you're looking for the most fragrant flowers, choose a plant with the largest blooms.

Plant Partners

These are some of the plants that can be combined together when Gardening:

Basil and Thyme- They are both cold-hardy plants and will grow well in shady areas.

Celery and Garlic- Both root vegetables that can be planted close to each other in the same soil and will help each other grow.

Tomato and Strawberry- These two are a great combination, they both need the same amount of sun exposure, space, water drainage, nutrients as well as temperature for optimal growth. They can also be grown together since they bloom at different seasons.

Carrot and Onion- These two are also a good combination to plant together, because they will help each other grow.

Cucumber and Beans- Cucumbers will need trellising, therefore the beans can grow on the trellis or fence instead.

Amaranth and Tomato- Both like similar conditions so planting them together will be beneficial for both plants.

Borage and Tomato- Both of them are effective in repelling pests as well as attract pollinators.

Chives and Mint- Both look good together in the garden.

Chicory and Carrot- These two work together in the garden. They both like similar conditions so planting them together will be beneficial for both plants.

Cornflower and Basil- These two are both annuals, they will need to be followed by other annual flowers to make sure that they don't get overgrown.

Cucumber and Strawberry- These two are a great combination, they both need the same amount of sun exposure, space, water drainage, nutrients as well as temperature for optimal growth. They can also be grown together since they bloom at different seasons.

Basil and Tomato- They are both good at repelling pests and will taste good when combined. Both also like a lot of sunlight.

Celery and Carrot- These two are a good combination since they will help each other grow.

Cornflower and Tomato- These two are a good combination since they grow well in similar conditions and both flower at different seasons.

Radish and Onions- They will grow well together, since the onions will attract fewer pests and radishes grow well with fewer nutrients.

Radish and Beans- The beans will help shade the radishes from the full sun exposure, helping them to grow better.

Corn and Beans- These two will grow well together since they are both legumes.

Cornflower and Beetroot- They are a great combination because they will repel pests alike, grow in similar conditions while also attracting pollinators.

Cabbage and Tomato- They are both root vegetables that can be planted close to each other in the same soil and will help each other grow.

Borage and Basil- Borage attracts bees which are essential to pollinate plants that would otherwise not produce fruit such as the basil, which is a flowering plant. They will also grow well together since they like similar conditions.

Celery and Mint- These two work well together in the garden. They both like similar conditions so planting them together will be beneficial for both plants.

Corn and Beans- These two will grow well together since they are legumes; they are both good at repelling pests.
Chickpea and Mint- Both dislike the same amount of sunlight and will grow well in shade. They can also be grown together since they bloom at the same time.
Fennel and Carrot- They work well together in the garden as they both repel pests, grow in similar conditions, and attract pollinators.
Cucumber and Garlic- These two work well together in the garden because they can repel pests alike and will also help each other grow.
Tomato and Onion- These two will grow best when placed close to each other since they will need to get a lot of sunlight. Both will also attract pollinators.
Radish and Cucumber- Both are good at repelling pests; they will grow well next to each other.
These plants are good to plant together, because they attract pollinators, grow in similar conditions and will also repel pests.

Organic gardening

Organic gardening is a set of techniques that promote earth health and crop yields. It relies on the natural nutrient sources already found in the soil, and on other organic substances such as compost to provide the growth nutrients. It also relies on crop rotation to prevent soil nutrients from becoming depleted.

Organic gardening began as a reaction to the increasingly industrialized methods of farming that came to dominate agriculture in the early 20th century. Its practitioners have been concerned about environmental degradation, especially the excessive use of non-renewable resources such as petroleum and natural gas, which are often used to power conventional farms. It prefers techniques that rely on human labor and management instead.

The term "organic" refers primarily to growing methods that work with nature, as opposed to against it. Organic gardening techniques incorporate elements such as companion planting, crop rotation, and the use of natural fertilizers. These techniques are intended to build soil fertility and control pests by encouraging natural ecosystems rather than to rely on synthetic chemicals.

A typical organic garden is maintained without the use of synthetic pesticides, herbicides, insecticides, and fertilizers. Not only does it help you grow healthy plants organically, but also good for your health.

Organic gardening techniques are often used in permaculture and greenhouse gardens, as well as for growing food plants. Organic horticulture is a well-established discipline, with numerous books and scientific publications available. Horticulturists specializing in organic gardening often have two to three years of college training in organic gardening principles, and may have additional training in plant pathology or entomology.

Benefits of organic gardening

1] Good for health: This organic gardening is not only good for growing plants, but it is also good for your health. The chemical fertilizers and pesticides used in non-organic gardening has been linked to a host of physical and mental problems including cancer, birth defects, and dizziness. The probability of getting these diseases is more if you are involved in the spraying process, or eating vegetables directly from the garden that has been sprayed with chemicals.

2] Better tasting vegetables: This organic gardening has been established long before the non-organic method and its taste is far better. It also allows your vegetable to retain more of their nutrients compared to non-organic methods.

3] Better nutrient density: Plants grown using organic fertilizers and weed killers retain more nitrates and phosphates than plants grown with synthetic chemicals. Also, they have been found to be packed with higher micronutrient levels.

4] Healthy soil: Organic gardening involves using compost and other organic matter in the soil, and that helps to build healthy soil. The soil becomes cleaner and healthier as a result of improving the soil with the use of organic fertilizers.

5] More beneficial microorganisms: Being exposed to higher levels of natural sunlight allows bacteria, fungi, protozoa, and other microorganisms to flourish in a better environment compared to that which occurs when you are growing your plants indoors. Also using organic pesticides results in the better growth of beneficial insects, which also means less harmful insects.

6] Easier to grow plants from seed: Another benefit of organic gardening is that the seeds are easy to grow if you are using organic methods. The seeds will sprout faster and quicker compared to using chemical fertilizers.

7] Consistent yield: Indoor gardening is usually inconsistent, but when you grow your plants outdoors, you get a more consistent yield. Also, weeds are kept at bay since chemicals do not kill them and it may even attract insects that eat those harmful weeds.

8] Better taste: The taste of the vegetables grown using chemical fertilizers and pesticides often has a bitter aftertaste. That is because they are not only used in too high doses, but they also have been rendered undrinkable by the chemicals. Such chemicals can also cause the crop to develop insects or even fungi that make it bitter in taste. That often results in throwing out a lot of produce.

9] Higher net profit: When comparing organic gardening and non-organic gardening, the former is cheaper to maintain since it does not require you to purchase chemicals. The vegetables are easier to grow and tend to have a higher yield. That means you will end up with more vegetables which results in higher profits.

10] Better quality soil: When using organic methods, the soil is not contaminated by toxic chemicals. This is because chemical fertilizers and herbicides/pesticides are not used in the soil. That means that you will have a better soil that will be productive for years.

11] Healthier plants: When you use natural methods, the plants become healthier as they receive nutrients and elements found in nature. The plant also becomes produce more vegetables, so you do not end up using too much pesticides or toxic chemicals to make them healthy.

12] Better vegetables: The vegetables that you use to grow your plants using organic methods are leaner, tastier, and have a higher amount of minerals than the ones grown with artificial fertilizers and chemicals.

13] You save money: By not using chemical fertilizers and pesticides you save money. It also means that you do not end up throwing out most of your produce because it is rotten or toxic. This is because the produce is high in vitamins and has nutrient levels that are much better than those produced by conventional methods.

14] You become more aware of the environment: When you do not use chemicals, your garden does not further contaminate the environment. Thus, you are more aware of how to take care of and maintain your garden.

15] You are able to harvest more produce: When using organic methods you can harvest a lot of vegetables from your garden compared to the natural methods, as a higher yield is possible. Also, when growing your vegetables organically it is easier to control pests and insects.

16] You avoid diseases: When spraying chemicals in your garden you can end up causing disease and illness to your plants. That means that there is a higher risk of plant diseases in an indoor garden compared to the organic garden since there are no pesticides used against insects or fungi.

17] Your plants are healthy: When you use natural fertilizers and weed killers, your plants are healthier and do not have any disease. They also grow at a faster rate since they are in a better environment with more sunshine.

18] There is less waste: When you use organic methods, you are more likely to harvest more vegetables since they thrive in the soil. Thus, there will be less waste as you can use your produce instead of throwing it away. Also, your budget for growing vegetables will not suffice as much since more vegetables are produced.

19] You are more confident: When you grow your plants with natural methods, you are much more confident as you know that they are not being harmed by the chemicals. That is because the fertilizers and pesticides you use do not harm any life form.

20] You become a better gardener: When plants grow in an organic environment they flourish and produce a lot of vegetables much better than the ones grown in an artificial environment. That means that you grow to become a better gardener since you are able to produce more and better vegetables.

21] It is a healthier lifestyle: When using natural methods for growing vegetables, there is no danger to your health. That is because the fertilizers and pesticides used in conventional methods are not only harmful to your plants but also to humans and animals. All of this makes it not only unhealthy but dangerous as well.

These are some of the advantages of using organic methods for growing your vegetables. You can use these advantages to further convince yourself that you should grow your vegetables organically and in turn save a lot of your money.

The Types Of Organic Gardening Suited For Your Home

The main types of organic gardening are: Container Gardening, Square Foot Gardening, Raised Beds Gardening and Traditional Crop Farming. Each type has advantages and drawbacks as well as its perfect applications for different climates and needs.

<u>Container Gardening</u>

It is a great choice for anyone who has limited space but still wants to grow vegetables and herbs in the garden. Containers are also a great way to start gardening if you have limited gardening experience or no experience at all. People typically plant in 6x6, 8x8, 10x10, 12x12, 16x16 and various other sizes depending on the size of their garden. It is possible to get creative and make your own containers out of just about anything!

<u>Square Foot Gardening</u>

It is a great way to maximize production from small spaces. With square foot gardening you grow your plants in rows instead of traditional rows. This preserves space and makes it easy to rotate crops around the garden. The crops are also easier to maintain and harvest because they are placed into small squares.

<u>Raised Beds Gardening</u>

It is a great solution for people who have limited space as well as people with poor soil. Raised beds allow you to grow vegetables without a large amount of space, and avoid the need to disturb the soil. This is helpful for new gardeners and those who want to save money on seeds and fertilizer by growing them organically in their own soil.

Traditional Crop Farming

This is considered the most common and easiest form of gardening. Traditional crop farming is growing vegetables and herbs the way they have been done for centuries. This method is not really organic but it can be used in an organic garden as well. The main benefit to this style of gardening is that you do not need a large area to grow a wide variety of crops.
These are just a few of the main forms of organic gardening, and as you can see it has a wide variety of benefits for anyone who wants to become an organic gardener.

What Will You Do With Your Organic Gardening At Home?

There are two main aspects of gardening that you need to focus on if you want to grow vegetables organically in your yard. You need to make sure that the soil is healthy and fertile, as well as the plants are resistant to pests and disease. If any of these things is off, then one pest or disease can ruin all of your hard work.
It's important to plant your garden in the right place the first time, as this would save you many troubles down the line. When you have any problems with your soil, then you'll need to consider how you can amend it and get it into a good condition. You may choose to either dig up some soil and add some new compost or manure to boost fertility levels, or if your soil is already healthy, then you can just top up the existing levels of organic matter in order to help maintain them.
When you're planning out your garden, you'll need to consider if it's possible for your whole kitchen garden to be completely organic. If you're planning on buying any plants at all then you'll need to make sure that you choose them from a reputable source, such as a garden center or nursery. You should always go for proven varieties of vegetables and fruit that are known to be resistant to disease.
When you plant out a vegetable garden, you should stick with one type of vegetable variety at a time and avoid growing more than one type of crop in the same plot. This is because it's very important to rotate your crops, so that pests and disease won't build up over time. If you don't rotate your crops then one plant will attract the pests of the other one, which can lead to a very big problem.
One of the best methods that you can fight off pests and disease in an organic garden is by using companion planting. If you grow certain types of plants next to each other, then they will help each other out by acting as a protective barrier against pests and disease.

How to plant a vegetable garden that is not toxic and all-natural.

Gardening is a great hobby. You can spend time outdoors away from noise and pollution while planting something to be proud of. But many people are worried about using chemicals in their vegetable garden, or have a space that can't handle the use of chemicals. It doesn't need to be this way! Check out these tips for gardening without using chemical pesticides or herbicides!

1. Start with a healthy soil that's rich in organic matter. This will help retain water and give plants the nutrients they need to grow strong and lush. The best method to do this is to make your own compost using things like food waste, grass clippings and leaves. Mulching with things like hay or straw will also add organic matter. Over time, you'll build up a healthy layer of topsoil that will help your garden thrive.
2. Buy seeds that are not genetically modified and organically grown. The reason why genetically modified seeds are becoming so popular is because they are engineered to produce a certain trait (like herbicide resistance). GMOs are not desirable in the vegetable garden.
3. Learn to look at a plant's roots and leaves to see if it's going to be resistant or sensitive to chemicals. This is very important because you don't want to use a chemical that will hurt your plants.
4. Use mulch on plants that are sensitive or weakened by chemicals, such as tomatoes. Mulching protects the roots by keeping weeds down, which helps prevent the spread of disease from plant-to-plant contact. It also creates a warmer microclimate where plants will be more likely to survive winter.
5. Try setting up a raised bed. This will make it harder for chemicals to get into the ground and harm your plants. The soil in a raised bed can also be used as compost to make the garden stronger and healthier.
6. Get rid of weeds by using weed killers that are not toxic to humans. Some organic weed killers are safe when used on flowers or edible plants, such as strawberries, tomatoes and lettuce. You can also use mulch to help control weeds.
7. Pick off bugs manually and destroy them so they don't spread to other crops.
8. Use natural barriers instead of chemical poisons. Instead of putting down poison, try spraying the leaves with a mixture of soap and water. This creates a layer on the leaves that will make it hard for bugs to get around. However, make sure you don't spray soap directly onto the plant or else it will die because of the lack of its protective cover.
9. Try to harvest your garden plants when they are ripe or about to be ripe so that you don't have to worry about insects, mold and other problems.
10. Get creative! You can plant herbs between your vegetables for added flavor and nutrition. Or you can grow flowers that act as a natural repellent.

Get to know your garden and take note of what's working or not working for you. This would help you make better decisions in the future.

Composting

Tips on starting compost pile for your gardening needs:
There are so many different methods to garden but some people, especially in the city, don't have access to dirt or a large enough backyard. If you enjoy gardening but lack an adequate space for it, then you should consider starting your own compost pile. This will help you to have access to fresh produce year round.
Pretty and practical
A well-maintained compost pile is easy to start, but it takes some time and attention each day. The compost pile will need a lot of space in the backyard. This can be any flat area where you can spread out the materials you have collected for your starter pile. You could create a garden bed using wooden or plastic bins. Another method is to lay down a tarp on the ground and pile up your supplies on top of that.
Once everything is organized, you have to water it every day until it is heated. This might take a few weeks depending on the size of the materials and how hot the weather is outside. There are different ways to heat your compost pile. You will need a thermometer and hot water, so that the compost pile will be heated to the right temperature. You can heat the compost by submerging it in water or by laying it in the sun.
When you have reached the perfect temperature for your compost pile (about 130°F), you can mix up all of your materials to form one uniform pile.
In compost pile gardening, the material you use to grow your plants is called organic fertilizer. Compost is a rich source of organic fertilizer and can be used to supply nutrients to your plants.
Nutrients like phosphorus, nitrogen and potassium are the main components of compost and are necessary for all plants. Giving your plants with the right amount of these nutrients helps them to grow and thrive.
Of course, not all plants need the same amount of nutrients. It is important to know what requirements your plants have before you plant them. Some examples of low nutrient-demand plants include most kinds of lettuce, spinach and carrots. On the other hand, there are high nutrient-demand plants such as tomatoes and azaleas which require more balanced nutrition in order to produce healthy flowers and fruits.
Many people like to compost all year round. If you plant a garden every year, then you will need to have a good supply of organic fertilizer. You can make more compost than the amount of time it takes for the plants in your garden. This means that there would always be new fresh organic fertilizer available for your plants.
If you do not have the time or financial resources to start your own garden, then you should consider starting a compost pile. This will give you access to fresh and healthy produce year round.
It is best to compost in the fall and spring. This is when it is easiest to start a compost pile because the weather is cool. However, it can be done year-round if you use your indoor space wisely.

The materials that are used for composting are divided into "browns" and "greens". The browns are the organic materials that you can find in your kitchen waste and yard waste. The greens are the plant-based materials that you have collected from your garden. These include any green grasses, leaves and flowers.

You have to assure that you have enough time to bring the composting materials up to a temperature that is about 130°F before use. This is what happens when plants use organic matter to create energy and grow healthy roots, stems and fruits.

When you're adding your composting materials to the pile, you should make sure they are wet first. This makes it easier for the compost to break down and be available for your plants. Too much water, however, could make your compost stick together which makes it harder to use later on.

Your composting materials don't have to be completely broken down when you use them in your garden. It is easier for plants to absorb organic matter when it is still a little bit chunky. After you have added the compost to your garden, you can use a tiller so that the compost will mix into the soil for better nutrient availability.

Composting is easy and a lot of fun especially if you're growing a garden every year. You will need to have good organic fertilizer so that your plants can grow healthy and strong. Composting is easy to do even if you live in an urban area. You just have to follow the guidelines from the materials you have collected. Composting helps you to have access to healthy and fresh produce every day all year round.

Some popular materials you can add into your composting are garden plants, sawdust, peat moss, grass clippings, and kitchen waste. You can also add manure and chicken manure to your compost pile as well. Manure is a significant source of nitrogen, which can be used in the soil to aid in plant growth.

Be sure to compost correctly for nutrients, because improper composting levels can actually harm your plants.

Steps in pile composting

These are the steps you have to follow when composting:

1. Sorting and Preparing Materials

First, you have to sort the different types of materials that you will use in your compost pile. The main materials will be compostable (browns) and non-compostable (greens). Sorting is the most important step in the composting process because it will help you get a more homogenous compost.

2. Balancing Your Materials

After sorting your materials, you will need to balance them. The browns should be about three times as much as the greens in order to create the right environment for composting. If it is too much of one or the other material, then your compost will not be able to break down properly and will be too wet or dry.

3. Adding Water

Adding water is important because it will make the compost work faster. Remember that you will need to have a good balance between water and trash materials so that you can get a proper mixture of both. If you do not add enough water, then your compost pile might break down faster than what is necessary while if you add too much water, then your organic trash will not be composted fast enough.

4. Turning Your Compost

It is important to turn your compost every week or so in order to help it break down properly. Turning the pile also helps equalize the moisture levels and keep the oxygen flowing through the pile for faster decomposition.

5. Using Your Compost

When you have enough compost ready, you can start using it in your garden or on your house plants. It is best to use the compost when it has been broken down but still has a little bit of texture to it.

6. Adding a Starter

You may also add a compost starter to your pile in order to speed things up. Compost starters are usually made from green materials such as kitchen scraps, grass clippings or vegetable trimmings. The important thing you need to look out for with compost starters is whether or not they have any harmful chemicals in them such as fertilizer so that you do not end up putting harmful chemicals into your garden or house plants.

7. Building Your Compost Pile

Your pile needs to be about 3 feet wide, 4 feet long and 3 feet tall in order to compost properly. Also, make sure it is in a level area that gets the right amount of exposure to the sun so that it can start composting as fast as possible.

8. Adding Air

To speed up the decomposition, you will need to make sure the compost pile is airy. This is the reason why it is essential to turn your compost every single week. The more oxygen your pile has, the faster it will decompose.

9. Maintaining Your Compost Pile

It is important to maintain your compost pile so that you can have a steady supply of compost for use in your garden and house plants. Make sure that you are turning your compost every week and start a new pile once you have used up the existing one so that there is always something ready to use.

10. Enjoy Your Compost

If your compost is ready, you can start using it in your garden or house plants. Just make sure not to put any chemicals in it to avoid harming your garden or house plants. Once you have finished with your compost, you can just use it later around the same area so that nothing will go to waste.

11. Adding Manure

You can also use manure for your compost as long as it is aged so that it is no longer smelly. If you are using manure, you will need to have a larger ratio of browns to greens since manure is much more potent.

12. Choosing the Right Spot for Your Compost Pile

In order to get the best results, make sure you select an area that gets enough sun so that your compost pile can start rotting faster than if it was in the shade. You will also want a flat area that is sturdy enough to hold your compost pile. If you are putting it in the garden, then you will want to make sure there is enough room for plant growth around it.

13. Diatomaceous Earth
Diatomaceous earth is also very good for getting rid of unwanted bacteria and fungi as well as mold so you will get the best results from your composting process.

14. Using Your Compost
Once the compost has broken down you may start using it in the garden or house plants. It is important to use it on a regular basis so that it always stays fresh and ready for use at all times. You can also add it to the soil in different areas of your yard or garden so that you have more organic matter to work with but remember to take care when using this material since it is very sharp and can cut you if you are not careful.

15. Airflow
It is important to make sure your compost has good airflow in order to break down properly. If your compost pile is small then you will need to turn it more often but if it is a large pile, then you might only have to turn it once every two weeks.

These are some very basic tips for making compost that you can use at home. They are simple and easy to follow and you will get great results that will make a difference in your garden or house plants. By following these tips regularly, you will start seeing your plants grow better and faster since they are acquiring all the nutrients that they need without the use of chemicals.

Tips on designing a raised bed for bigger gardening yield.

The most important matter to consider when designing a raised bed is the soil. If you are working with artificial soil, it will be better if you layer it with compost and fertilizer to help the plants grow easily. If your soil consists of organic matter, simply mix that with some sand and you should be good.

Finding good wooden or metal frames can also be a challenge due to their exorbitant cost, so here are some methods you can get around this problem:

Use old pallets. Cut off the top of them and then place these on the ground to store. Then, make use of these by stacking wooden planks on top of them. Place a layer of soil around it and then add some bricks to the outside edges to prevent slugs from getting to your vegetables.

Plant stakes or bamboo poles in your raised bed. These will not only give support for the frame but also prevent weeds from growing around it.

When working with concrete, you should never place it directly on or in the soil. A good way to solve this is by using an old pallet with a layer of soil, and another layer of hardened concrete on top of it.

You should also consider the depth of your beds. The deeper the bed, the bigger the benefits will be. The size should also be decided by the size of your plants and how much space you have for them to grow.

The height of your beds should be several times the diameter of the plants they are intended for. It will allow for better airflow and will help prevent weeds growing up from the soil around it.

If you have a well- producing garden, then you should consider using a layer of plastic underneath your raised beds. This will help prevent ants from entering the soil and prevent them from climbing up to the plants and stealing their leaves and flowers.

When you are working with a small area such as a balcony or patio, you can use several bamboo poles and plant stakes to make the space bigger.

Finally, you should consider plants that will not need a lot of nutrients. Some plants work best when they receive less water and sunlight than others. These include tomatoes, peppers, eggplants and herbs that will turn beautiful colors when used in mixed planters.

Mulching

Mulching is gardening techniques that can help plants grow healthier and stronger. Plants need certain nutrients, such as nitrogen, potassium and phosphorus to grow. These nutrients are taken up with water from the soil and usually make their way into the plant's leaves to be converted into food. However, when heavy rains come and wash away those important nutrients in the soil, mulching provides a slow release of nutrients directly to the roots.

Mulches can be made out of organic materials like straw, leaves, hay and wood chips. However, the organic ingredients are not always beneficial to plants. Straw is more beneficial because of its ability to retain moisture throughout its lifespan. The best way to use mulches is to add them to the top one-third of the soil. Not only will this help slow down water runoff, but adding it near the surface will also allow for quicker and easier penetration through the soil by certain bacteria and fungi that help plants absorb nutrients faster.

The perfect time to add mulch is after the soil temperature has increased to above 50 degrees Fahrenheit (10 degrees Celsius). This would allow the bacteria and fungi to use the nitrogen and other nutrients that were previously lost in the soil. If you are using organic materials, and are unsure of how organic they are, try composting them first. Mulching also can help protect plants from pests like slugs and snails. These pests lose much of their moisture when they slither or slide over the top of a mulch. They do not have enough water to breed in the soil because it is protected by the mulch. A mulch also helps protect plants from extreme weather conditions, such as too much sun and wind, or too little water. It also helps regulate the soil temperature, keeping it cooler in hot weather and warmer in cold weather, without letting the plants' roots freeze.

Mulch is not just for use in gardens. It also helps inhibit weed growth, providing an easier way to keep your garden weed free. Mulching can provide a natural form of pest control, keeping away most insects and worms from eating your plants. Insects and worms can eat the organic ingredients in mulches, which in turn can kill them.

Mulch isn't a great ingredient for adding nutrients back into the soil, since it does not hold moisture like soil does, and it's also hard to harvest. The best mulches are those made of organic materials like straw, wood chips, and leaves. These materials hold in water as well as nutrients.

How to prepare mulch:

You can create your own mulch mix from readily available locally abundant low quality (waste) organic material such as:

It is best not to include a substantial amount of animal manures e.g. cow, horse, sheep, pig etc., or manure from any animal intended for human consumption, since this may lead to disease risks and products that are not acceptable in markets. However some dairy cattle manure can be used on acid loving plants such as blueberries.

For good quality mulch add bulking agents such as perlite, pumice, crushed corn cobs or coir. These materials will lighten the mulch by increasing volume, improve the drainage and increase the air content.

Use small particle sizes of woody organic material such as sawdust or bark chips that will break down quickly. Avoid coarse textured materials that can inhibit root penetration.

Depending on the specific requirements and fertility status of the soil, local availability of materials, cost and other market opportunities a mix of materials can be used for mulching such as:

Eucalyptus leaves are an ideal mulch to use in fruit tree orchards. They are high in potassium content and other nutrients. They also suppress weed growth.

Non-woody organic material such as shredded leaves, straw, grass clippings etc. are also used for mulching. However they may not be available in large quantities or even at all areas of the country. Therefore these materials cannot be easily replaced and will need to be considered part of the cost of production.

A mulch layer allows for quick moisture transport through the soil profile and greater soil moisture retention than bare earth or a traditional garden bed. It also provides a temporary habitat for beneficial insects such as ground beetles, spiders and ladybirds. Mulch layers can be made out of many different materials. These include: waste green material, wood shavings, wood chips, straws, sawdust and grass clippings. These materials have advantages and disadvantages. Shredded leaves are a high quality mulch when they are mixed with compost they degrade rapidly while straw is coarse in texture, which can cause soil compaction if too much is used. Sawdust and wood chips are preferred in the colder areas of the UK, because these materials hold more heat than straws and grass-clippings. Wood shavings are also used in colder areas since they are more resistant to moisture loss.

Mulches not only reduce planting costs as they protect the soil from erosion, evaporation, leaching and weed growth but also suppress weed competition. They break down into organic matter over time and improve soil structure through increased microbial activity. This improves aeration and water-holding capacity, increases soil fertility and helps with drainage.

The use of mulch can lower the need to use herbicides, insecticides, fungicides and fertilizers in a mix since it provides an effective means of controlling weeds and pests without using these chemicals. It also helps control diseases by providing an environment where beneficial organisms are able to survive. This also prevents weed seeds from being able to germinate when the soil is bare.

Mulching is not only beneficial to gardening but also for organic farming practices as well. Organic farming is a way of growing food where you don't use pesticides or synthetic fertilizers. Instead, you can use natural or organic fertilizers and use mulch as your pest control.

Urban Gardening

Urban gardening is a relatively new concept. It began in the 1960's as a response to the growing concern over pollution and food security. In fact, one of the most popular urban gardeners, Ruth Stout, was living in Manhattan when she started writing about her experiences with keeping a garden on her fire escape.

In recent years, urban gardening has evolved into a cultural movement based on how people are growing their own produce and "tending their own containers" (to quote Michael Pollan). People are doing this for a number of reasons. Some do it because they need to minimize their carbon footprint and eat healthier food. Others do it just for fun. And others do it because they are worried about our food supply and want to take back control of their food source.

Urban gardening is a way for people, especially city dwellers, to reconnect with the earth and interact with nature by providing for themselves instead of always depending on others to provide their food. Urban farming is a way to grow plants in public space. This is usually done by planting fruit trees, beets, or other food crops that can be harvested on a regular basis and can be used for cooking or eaten fresh. However, urban farming doesn't have to be limited to just growing food. Sometimes people will grow herbs such as thyme which they make into herbal ointments for healing.

Urban Gardening using Organic method

The benefits of urban gardening include soil conservation, food security, climate change mitigation, economic self-reliance and community building. But there are also health and environmental reasons for doing this kind of work. By tending to your own garden, you reduce the need for transportation (from farm to store), packaging (which reduces waste) and pesticides/herbicides (which may be cancer causing or toxic).

Urban gardening with organic methods is healthier because you are able to control what goes on around your garden. You can choose which fertilizers and pesticides you put in the ground and thus apply only those which are proven safe, non-toxic, and not cancer-causing. Organic gardening is also beneficial to the environment because it cuts down on carbon emissions as well as the pollution which is caused in transit from farm to store. You can choose an organic garden to grow your own food, herbs, or medicinal plants. You can also apply the principles of organic gardening when you are working on land that was previously given over to industrial purposes such as mining or dumping.

There are basically five methods of urban gardening with organic methods that you can use. These are referred to as intensive, semi-intensive, extensive, thoughtful, and creative gardening. This refers to how many square feet of grow space you have in the garden. A more intensive method of gardening with organic methods would be planting a lot of food crops such as tomatoes or peppers whereas a less intensive method would be a herb garden or just planting one food crop such as tomatoes.

In an intensive garden you will probably be planting more food plants than any garden that you maintain without organic methods. In the semi-intensive method of gardening, you will plant fewer food plants and lots of herbs. And in the extensive method you can plant as many as possible without negatively impacting the land. The thoughtful method is just a serious "how to" book for vegetable gardening with organic methods which can be used throughout the season for whatever vegetables are growing on your land. And the creative method of gardening with organic methods is just a set of rules with which you can determine some guidelines for how you want to garden in an urban setting.

Urban Gardening Techniques with Organic method

The average city lot produces more than enough food to feed a family of four and yet, nearly half the world's population live in cities. In these urban settings, many people lack access to a backyard or other green space where they can grow their own food.
Many people with limited space find it intimidating to get started with urban gardening. If this sounds like you, there are many reasons you should consider getting started right away.
When you don't have a green thumb and don't know a tomato plant from a zucchini squash plant, there's no need to worry. All of the plants need little care and can be grown in containers on your balcony or patio, even if your space is limited to a windowsill.
Urban gardening can be an eco-friendly way to get more vegetables into your diet. Buying fresh, organic produce from local farmers can reduce the amount of pesticides and chemicals that may be on your food, which is especially important for children's health.
Even if you already have a garden you tend to forget about during the winter months, you can start an urban garden any time of year. The benefits include the ability to grow your own produce without outside watering or caretaking. If your family does some cooking from home during the winter months, gardening also provides a way to grow crops that are in season during those cold months.
These are different kinds of urban gardening with organic method:

Raised bed farming:

This method is very simple. It involves building beds with wood or concrete blocks that are approximately 24 inches high. You can make your raised bed as a rectangle, which is the easiest shape to build, or you may use other shapes such as a circle or even a leaf shape.
The good thing about this urban gardening technique is that you can use any soil and don't have to spend additional money on acquiring new soil. However, you should keep in mind that some kinds of plants thrive better in certain kinds of soil. If you like to grow vegetables, don't use potting soil. You can use compost-enriched soil that is designed especially for gardening.
As you bury the planting medium, it transforms into a mini-forest of vegetation. This is why it's important to have the right kind of plant as a base in your raised bed.

Vegetable garden:

This is the classic kind of gardening, where you can grow all kinds of vegetables in your container. If you don't have more space, it's still possible to have a vegetable garden. Many people use hanging baskets to grow their vegetables. You can also plant vegetables in small pots on your balcony or patio.

The brilliant thing about growing your own vegetables is that you know exactly what goes into each plant and there are no chemicals used to grow them. You need to make sure that your container is large enough to accommodate the vegetables. Also, make sure that the soil is just the right temperature and pH level. You can have a controlled environment in your container so that you can grow fruits and vegetables year round.

To own your own urban gardening is very beneficial to your health because you get fresh organic vegetables without having to go to a grocery store. The only thing you need is a garden container where you can grow your crops.

Microgreen farming:

Microgreens are the young and just sprouted seedlings of vegetables. For example, if you want to grow microgreens, you can start with a cabbage plant. When the cabbage plant is young, about 4 inches tall, you can cut it off at the base and submerge it in water. Dark cover to go over the soil in your garden during its growth cycles. There are three types of soil that can be used for this process: clay, peat moss and vermiculite. Then spray bottle to mist the water onto the plants.

When you're ready to begin planting, be sure to choose the type of microgreen seeds that you will be using. A good choice is a mixture of broccoli, carrot, chard, clover, and radish seeds. These can all be planted at once, but they should have separate rows so that they are each spaced far enough apart for air to pass through and allow for proper growth. Microgreens are very nutritious because they retain all of the nutrients that aren't processed by a mature plant. They are good source of vitamins and minerals for your diet. You can extend the life of your microgreens by storing them in the refrigerator with a moist paper towel. If you like to make some sandwiches, you can grow microgreens in your kitchen because they are so easy to maintain.

Vertical gardening:

You can build structures or fences around your home in order to grow food vertically. This type of gardening is great if you have very limited space. You can grow anything on a fence such as beans, cucumber, squash, peas and other vegetables.

You don't need any special tools to start vertical gardening. If you already have a fence, you can grow your own vegetables on it. If you don't have any fencing, you can build a simple structure using wooden planks. If you don't want to use wood, you can also use concrete blocks or even bricks.

When you choose the method of urban gardening that is best for your family, it's important to grow crops that are in season at your local farmers' market. You can buy organic seedlings so that they are not sprayed with pesticides.

Square foot garden:

This method helps you to grow your own vegetables in a small area. You can also grow vegetables in a small area if you have a courtyard or balcony that you want to farm. The organic method in square foot gardening is to use a garden soil that is rich in nutrients.

A Square foot Garden is a type of garden design that divides the plant growing area into square shapes separated by pathways. The idea is that you'll dedicate one square to each garden variety, growing only one thing in each square. Use a spade to dig each area 12 inches deep, and then fill the hole with compost. The most common vegetables grown in square foot gardens are lettuce, peas, radish, turnips, cabbage, corn, tomatoes and peppers. On top of the ground cover special organic fertilizers that will help the soil retain moisture for longer periods of time.

Container garden:

This is a great method for novice gardeners to start farming at home. The only thing that you need is a container where you can grow your vegetables. In as much as the container has drainage holes, it will work for the container gardening method. You can grow tomatoes, peppers, carrots and other vegetables in a large pot on your balcony or backyard. You can also build a vertical frame around your container if you want to get several tiers out of it.

Container gardening is very beneficial when you use organic methods in a small space. For example, you can grow a vine that can cover several tiers of your container garden. It's very easy to build and plant this type of garden because all you need is a large pot and some organic soil.

No dig garden:

Are you tired of tilling your garden every year? If you are, then this method is perfect for you. You don't even have to dig up the soil to use this type of gardening! It's a great idea if you want to protect your backyard by not digging it up.

What makes no-dig gardening so easy is that all you need is a container where you can grow several crops. You can start your vegetable garden with peas and beans because they provide great nitrogen for the soil. The main reason that this type of gardening is so popular is that it's completely organic and it's also simple to build.

These are only some of the organic gardening methods that you can use to start farming at home. You'll be able to grow your own crops by following these tips and using some of your time to do it!

With organic gardening, the soil is protected from many environmental factors that could potentially damage your soil. You can also grow large crops using this method without tilling the soil or using inorganic fertilizers.

Tips on planting a Garden at home

The first few weeks of spring can be a bit uninspiring when it comes to the weather, but with a little enthusiasm and some time outdoors, you can make sure your yard has plenty of color this year.
Here are a few quick plant care tips for your garden:
#1. Check the soil
The first step in getting a new garden started is to make sure you have a healthy patch of soil to work with. A balanced, fertile mixture that retains water and nutrients will provide your garden with adequate nourishment for healthy growth.
#2. Soil Preparation
Dig up your garden beds a few weeks before planting. Turn over the soil using a shovel, breaking up any clumps of dirt or rocks that may be present. This will assure that your plants get enough amount of soil to work with as they grow.
#3. Planting Your Garden
Plant in rows or blocks rather than in haphazard groups for easier maintenance later on. Plant seeds or plants of the same family together in alternating rows or blocks.
#5. Watering
Water your garden for at least once a day during the growing season and every two to three days in winter. Keep a plastic bag handy for collecting excess water that can help keep the soil from becoming waterlogged and allow it to drain easily.
#6. Mulching
A layer of mulch may be beneficial to prevent weeds from growing or to add nutrients by providing living roof coverings for your plants.
#7. Weed Control
Weeds are having competition with your plants for nutrients and space, which can cause your garden to produce more weeds than it does flowers, fruits or vegetables. The best method to deal with weeds is to pull them out as soon as they appear—don't wait until the weeded plants are over 3 inches tall, as that's when they may become tough or bitter tasting.
#8. Watering & Fertilizing
After the leaves have lost their color, stop watering and fertilize again. The leaves of most plants will die if watered too often, so it is best to water only when the soil is dry.
#9. Fertilizing:
Fertilizer is the biggest factor in whether or not your garden produces crops. The best way to feed your plants or trees is with a well balanced fertilizer that provides what they need plus a little extra for good measure. Check for a fertilizer's ratio, which will be listed on the packaging, to insure that you are using it correctly.
#10. Pruning:
Pruning helps in maintaining the health and vigor of plants and trees. Remove all weak or dead branches to promote new growth.
#11. Pests and Diseases
Some garden pests cannot be avoided; however, you can decrease their numbers by keeping your garden healthy with regular care and fertilizing. Diseases can be controlled by planting resistant varieties and maintaining overall good garden health.

#12. Fall Vegetables:

Hardiness: The yellow summer squash, pumpkins and zucchini are frost tender and require a well-built cold frame to head them over during the winter months. The tomatoes (except for varieties with resistance) can be set out in October if you live in a weather that gets below freezing temperatures.

Protect your new garden from possible frost damage with cold frames, greenhouses, black plastic or wooded windbreaks.

#13. Harvesting:

Harvest most of your vegetables and fruits by hand; except for harvesting tomatoes and pumpkins, which should be harvested with a sickle.

#14. Planting New Seedlings:

Plant seedlings as soon as the soil could be worked in the garden or in pots outside. Plant in well-drained soil, 6 inches apart on centers that are slightly raised above the ground to help keep the plants upright during transplanting. Water with a light application of water, and keep the soil evenly moist.

#15. Planting New Pots:

Plant new pots in a sunny spot with well-drained soil, and keep the soil evenly moist. Plant no deeper than two inches. Use six-inch pots for the larger lettuces and nine-inch pots for the smaller varieties.

These are the basic essentials for growing a garden at home. There are many other things that one must keep in mind while getting started. The list above should be a guideline for the novice gardener.

Garden Maintenance and Pruning

Maintaining and pruning a flower garden is an important factor if you want to keep your plants healthy. Flower gardens require regular care to remain abundant and beautiful, so read on if you're interested in learning more about gardening!

But what exactly goes into maintaining a flower garden? Well, there are many different tasks that need to be taken care of. Let's start with watering the plants, since lack of moisture can cause damage that is irreversible. If you don't believe that, then look at ancient civilizations around the world. For example, some of the most famous Chinese buildings are monuments to how man-made structures can be seriously weakened by lack of moisture.

While some plants can survive without regular watering (depending on their kind) others cannot, and will wither and die if not properly taken care of. Therefore, it's best to keep your plant life hydrated by watering them regularly. You can measure the amount of moisture in the soil by sticking your finger into the earth. If it's dry, then it's time to water them. If not, then you might want to wait a couple more days before watering them again.

About once a month, you should prune your plants so that they stay healthy and strong. Even though it might seem cruel to cut off some of your plant life, you'll actually be doing more good than harm by pruning them. It's a simple process that involves cutting from the base of the plant. You'll know it's time to prune when you begin to see dead or dying leaves on certain plants.

It may seem silly, but pruning can really make a big difference in your plant life. Not only does pruning help keep them healthy and strong, but it also helps your flowers and fruits to grow bigger.

As for fertilizing your plants, you should do that once a week. You could give them a boost by using liquid fertilizer or slow-release pellets. Just sprinkle the fertilizer around the base of your plants, and they will be all set!

If you follow these guidelines for maintaining and pruning your flower garden, then you'll be able to keep things running evenly and keep your garden looking healthy and vibrant!

How to take care of your garden

Gardening could be a very rewarding hobby, but it's also one of the more challenging ones. To be sure you get off to a good start, here are some of our best tips for maintaining your garden:

- Clear fallen leaves from your lawn regularly.
- Apply a fertilizer formulation after watering your plants.
- Apply all liquids in the direction of the foliage, for optimal absorption.
- If you are planning on moving your garden around your home, dig up the roots and replant at the new location. This will reduce transplant shock and ensure your plants grow to their full potential in their new location.

- Cover any exposed roots with mulch, this will prevent them from drying out during the summer months.
- Make sure to change out your water often, especially if you're using a watering can.
- The best time of day to water your garden is early morning or late afternoon; early morning is best because all the water has a chance to evaporate during the heat of the day, and late afternoon lets the water soak in during cool evening hours.
- When planting seeds be sure to plant them at least one inch deep and keep them well watered.
- For larger plants, like trees, it is best to delay replanting your garden for at least one year. This will allow the root system to fully establish and any debris on the surface of the ground can be removed using a power lawn mower.
- Before planting any new plantings, remove all existing structures from these areas so that if there are problems with these plants they will not affect other parts of your landscaping.
- Avoid planting any trees, bushes, or other plants near power lines.
- If you are trying to grow a specific flowering or fruiting plant, be sure to buy a plant that is already on its way towards maturity. These are usually labeled as "established plants" in the nursery.
- If you are trying to grow a perennial plant, try to plant it after the last frost. This will allow it to establish well before a frost kills it.
- For the best results when planting bare root plants, strive to plant them in full sunlight. Plants with heavy foliage will require shade if they are planted in these conditions.
- Avoid planting your plants too deeply; roots should be at least half an inch below the soil level.
- If you are planting a new tree, shrub, or plant with fruit, it is a good idea to give it about six weeks of total rest before planting it. This will allow the root system to grow and help produce a healthy plant
- Dig up and remove any existing weed seeds that may be near your intended plants during planting time.
- When planting "fruiting" plants, avoid planting them too close to other fruiting plants. This can cause these "incompatible" plants to become inbred, resulting in fruit that is mostly seed and very little actual fruit.
- When planting new woody cuttings of trees or shrubs, cut them at an angle to make sure the plant will grow properly. Simply cutting the plant straight down can cause it to develop very weak roots and not survive as well as a healthy one.
- After planting your seedlings, make sure to place a well-cared for tree in the ground so the roots can develop a good structure.
- Lily of the valley is a brilliant choice for herb gardening; it attracts many beneficial insects, which will help to keep pests away from your plants.

- If you are planting any herb seeds, be careful with their spacing. They can be very sensitive and too much space between beds may cause them to become inbred and not produce the best results.
- When planting any type of seed production, be sure to separate the male plants from the female plants. The male plants will wither and die when they do not have access to a female plant.
- After you have planted your seeds, place a plastic sheet over the soil. This would help retain moisture in the soil and prevent blowouts from wind or water splashing on the soil.
- When you have so many weeds in your garden, lay down some mulch around your garden and this will suppress weed growth.
- Be sure to mulch your plants with an organic mulch; this will create a healthier environment for your plants and will help decrease the need for pesticides to be used.

Tips on pruning your plants for a better and healthier growth.

Pruning is a therapeutic process that helps in improving the overall health condition of your plant. Here are the reasons why you should prune your plants:

1. Helps with healthy growth and appearance of the plant.
2. Helps with disease control.
3. Reduces risk of pests.
4. Prevents damage from wind and sun.
5. Readily available at most gardening centers or nurseries in various sizes and shapes for different types of plants and climates.
6. Cost effective.

Pruning your trees and shrubs is a rewarding experience. It makes them look presentable by getting rid of excess branches, removing diseased or damaged wood and maintaining their shape. The succeeding tips would help you maintain your plants in excellent shape:

1. Trim off any broken or diseased branches or those that hang low over window sills or below power lines.
2. Trim dead branches back to a point above an outward growing branch and flush with the main branch above it if they aren't brittle.
3. Cut back all but the topmost branches on young trees and those that are growing away from the trunk.
4. Trim off spent canes or old growth of younger trees to make the tree look full, bushy and neat.
5. Trim off any dead or sickly looking leaves.
6. Strip away dead, diseased or broken wood on larger trees to prevent diseases from moving up into healthy branches and causing further damage.
7. Prune off all the dead or diseased wood on shrubs and hedges.
8. Trim off all winter-damaged wood on smaller trees to prevent them from becoming weak in the spring.
9. Prune off any damaged or broken branches and those that are touching each other or other branches.

10. Trim back shrubs periodically to encourage new growth from the trunks while keeping them at a reasonable size for their species in relation to the garden space they occupy.
11. Trim off the main stem above a lateral branch to encourage the lateral branch to become the main branch in its place.
12. Cut back the branches of evergreen shrubs spent flowering and fruit to new growth each spring, trimming off any that are growing sufficiently.
13. Cut down shrubs if they have started to become leggy or if they are crowding other plants in your garden bed.
14. Cut back perennial shrubs and annuals when they have gone dormant to encourage new growth in the spring.
15. Never cut off large branches of young trees when you want them to stay bushy, such as on a corner, to encourage side growth or to keep it presentable in its current pot.
16. When taking cuttings from large shrubs to make new plants, leave one bud on the branch and take away the rest so that the cutting will have enough root mass for success.
17. Prune off any flowering shoots to prevent them from becoming flower heads.
18. Prune back plants that are crowding the boundaries of their pots or borders to give them room to grow.
19. Prune back branches and foliage away from the center of a branch to encourage all the others to fill in more evenly around it.
20. Cut off oldest brother branches so that emerging buds can be exposed and receive proper light, water and fertilizer as they develop into new branches.

Pest and Disease Control

The best gardening techniques for dealing with pests, bugs, and diseases without using any harmful chemicals. It will also tell you how they can be prevented in the first place so that they don't become a problem.

A disease is a sickness or weakness in a plant. When the disease is mild, usually the plant can heal itself. When it becomes worse, it can destroy your whole crop or garden.

Symptoms of diseases appear when the disease has been present for at least 7 days. To treat them you will need to identify what they are first and then use fungicides to control or eliminate them.

Any plant anyone wants to grow can be infected with some kind of disease. One or two diseases could get into your garden and destroy the whole crop of plants. It is very important to know the cause of diseases to avoid them in the first place, but you may also use chemicals to control them if they become a problem.

Using only potash, wood ashes, or compost to control diseases is a good idea. Compost also helps the plants to build up resistance against certain diseases.

Harmful fungus, bacteria and virus affect your plants and lower your crop's production levels. The chemicals used for these diseases need to be applied before any symptoms appear on the plant. Fungus grows slowly so it makes it easier for you to identify them and remove them right away when you know what to look for.

Chemical is a substance that is not a plant, "organic" or in a small amount, any pesticide you use to control insects, weeds and diseases should be used only under certain conditions or you can become more vulnerable to pests. The pesticides available in the market are harmful to people and pets so that's why it's better to use organic sprays to control some of the small insects such as aphids for example.

If you want to use chemicals then deep plant watering should be avoided. Use shallow watering or rain water to avoid the growth and hiding places of pests.

Using organic sprays or simply compost, you can prevent insects that could cause diseases on your plants. Composting makes it easier to control certain insects like ants. Taking a bath, massage with herbal oils, and using essential oils from your garden can also help you.

When you are a new gardener you will find this very helpful in understanding the nature of plants and how to control them without using harmful chemicals.

Fungus- Botrytis is so mild you probably won't notice it. Only when the black mold covers the whole plant, it is a sign that this is the beginning of botrytis.

<u>Botrytis-</u> The first signs are really small brown dots that appear on the leaves and slowly they get bigger until they leave black/brown spots all over your plant or garden.

To prevent this disease you need to keep your garden free of dead leaves and infected plants (do not compost them). Keep your garden watered properly and in a good condition. Cover your plants with nets to protect them from being infected by the botrytis.

If you have this disease on your plant then you will have to remove all of the affected parts and disinfect them with chemical fungicides or use organic methods to get rid of this disease.

<u>Fungi, mushrooms-</u> As for fungi, they can seriously damage the whole plant, unlike Botrytis which only attacks single leaves. When you notice any brown spots on the leaves, it is a good sign to apply fungicides.

<u>Molds</u> can be a serious problem for plants because of the spores that are released during molds growth. There are many variety of molds that may cause diseases and they can spread to other plants if you let your garden to stay like this.

To prevent these diseases use chemical fungicides or organic methods such as compost, plant oils, baked white bread and strawberries. In fact, using a mixture of all these can help you to control the disease.

<u>Disease signs:</u>

Black spots on leaves

Frequently diseased plants, insects, and animals are those that are not allowed to get near your garden. If you keep your garden clean and give it good nutrients and water then this is the best way to do it.

If you see other insects or animal in your garden then keep them isolated from your garden so they do not carry diseases to your plants.

If you see this disease on your plant then you need to identify the cause of it. Determine if this is caused by insects or molds or fungus. Apply organic methods and chemical fungicides to it.

Pesticide-

This is a harmful chemical that will kill the healthy plants and cause them to die. Pesticide can be used for controlling pests such as pests of corn, pumpkins, strawberries, peppers, squash, etc...

Before using pesticide on your plants, you need to know that this chemical will kill the healthy plants and not the ones that already get sick.

If you see these signs on your plants then it is better to use organic methods such as compost, plant oils and baking white bread to keep your soil clean.

If you use pesticides in your garden then be sure to cover them well with a plastic sheet or leaves (to keep them from drying out) so that they do not get exposed to rain and sun.

If you have to use chemical fungicides then be sure to check the instructions and the precautions before using them.

It is always better to use organic methods for keeping your garden clean and preventing diseases.

How to avoid diseases:

Avoid insects- Like we said, pests can spread diseases, so if you want your plants and garden healthy then keep them safe from these insects. Use insecticides such as oils, hot pepper spray and so on...

If you have some insect that is a problem for your plants then it is better to isolate them from your garden.

Organic methods-

This is available from health food store and organic garden center. It consist of plant's seeds. You can grow herbs such as basil, rosemary, thyme, mint etc... or you can even grow vegetables like tomatoes, peppers, radishes and so on...

Mix the organic material with your soil and water it well. This will keep your plants healthy and it is a good way to treat bacteria, fungi and mold.

If you have some diseased plant then cut them off and throw them in the compost to prevent the rest of your garden.

Store those seeds in a cool, dry area such as freezer or refrigerator.

You can also dry out strawberry seeds for two or three weeks at 80-120 °F before storing them away until spring planting season.

Assure that the seeds you are planting are fresh. Do not mix old seeds with new ones or dry out old seeds before storing.

Insects and diseases-

When you notice these insects in your garden then it is better to use organic methods such as compost, plant oils and baking soda to keep your soil clean and healthy.

Choose plants that are resistant to pests or diseases, such as onions, potatoes, broccoli, lettuce and garlic.

If you use pesticides then be sure to cover them well with a plastic sheet (to keep them from drying out) so that they do not get exposed to rain and sun. Avoid using chemical fungicides unless you need to.

Isolation-

If you are growing plants that are diseased or infected then isolate them from other healthy plants in your garden or potting area. Keep your healthy plants away from unhealthy plants with the help of garden netting.

Use garden blueberry bags to isolate runner beans so that they don't contaminate other plants while they are in bloom.

Plants can be grown in a pot and moved to another spot when there is an outbreak of a disease or pest. Just make sure that you are not moving healthy plants with the diseased ones. If you have to move them in smaller quantities then it is better to use newspaper or black plastic bags.

Diseases and pests can be prevented by not watering or fertilizing them too much.

This is how I keep my tomatoes pest-free, I usually apply minced garlic on my tomato plants covered with plastic bags.

Another way to deal with these pests is by using a bag of insect killers to deter them from your garden. Apply the insecticide once in 4 -6 weeks to prevent damage from weeds.

If you are searching for a healthy alternative then consider growing your vegetables in pots instead of beds. Pots take less space and you will be able to move them easily to different parts of the house.

If you have the patience then consider planting some flowers around your tomato plants. I assure you, these tomato growing tips will help in increasing your yield.

Growing your own food

It's no secret that we have gained a lot by forgetting to take care of our planet. But it is also a well-known reality that, in order to save and preserve our environment, we need to start including the idea of sustainability into our everyday life. This idea, if applied through gardening, has been proven by many studies as an increasingly effective way to combat the soaring rates of global warming and ecological degradation.
It's not just about the food. It's about a sense of freedom and self-reliance, the thrill of nurturing and watching life - even for just a few minutes - grow out of something you've tended to so carefully. It's about time-honored traditions and family ties, as well as the adventure of new food experiences.
There is no greater gift than what you can provide to yourself by growing your own garden, with patience, hard work, and some careful planning.
The rewards are easily two to three times greater than the time and effort that go into growing vegetables in a garden.
You can, if you choose, grow all your own food for yourself, your family and friends. You can have it fresh and flavorful throughout the year since you know everything comes directly from your garden. Even if you don't have space for a garden on your lot or in your yard, you can still get fresh food every week by growing it at home. And you'll never pay for anything you don't eat. If your budget is tight, you can stretch your money by growing food in pots indoors, then when the weather permits, transplanting to your garden. You can choose to grow only your own produce, or you can grow a little cash crop for sale. If you must have something else in your garden besides fruits and vegetables (such as flowers), there are other ways to get the added income and the experience of growing other herbs, vegetables, potatoes, chiles, etc.
As we all know, food is the only thing that lets us live. A healthy diet is also necessary to maintain our vitality. So from now on, you will always remember that a healthy diet is not synonymous with fast or cheap food, but with organic food.
One of the benefits of a sound and balanced diet is that it can be accomplished in an easy and convenient way. So, if you dream of fresh, natural and organic food, all you need for this is a patch of land and a little bit of sunshine.
However, if you are one of those people who would rather buy their organic food instead of growing it, please note that it is always worth giving gardening a try. You might be amazed by how much money can you save by growing your own vegetables in your backyard.
Even if you are living in a crowded city, there is always a chance that you can grow something. A lot of people around the world began gardening without even realizing it. You may have already planted a few flowers or vegetables in your small garden at home, or maybe you've just watered some plants on the balcony. Even when you don't think about it, this is still gardening.

How to buy seeds for a healthy garden

All gardeners have a list of their favorite plants. These green thumb enthusiasts will spend hours selecting seeds from the shelves at the nursery for their next harvest. But there are some mistakes that novice gardeners should avoid when purchasing seeds to ensure they do not spoil crops in their garden and lose money.

These are some tips on how to buy seeds for healthy plants:

<u>Buy from a quality provider</u>. There are many different seed sellers on the market, but only a few of them have been proven over time, as being the best providers when it comes to healthy plants. And don't buy from farms and seed companies that take advantage of people with low literacy skills. They'll sell you a bag of seeds for a cheaper price, but it might not be full or even have any seeds at all.

<u>Order early</u>. When you're thinking of starting to build your own garden this year, then order the seeds early. Online retailers will often offer specials and discounts if you place an order for multiple bags or items, so take advantage of that. And if you need multiple bags of seeds to start the garden, then you could save a lot of money by ordering them at the same time.

<u>Buy bulk.</u> Buying seeds in bulk is a great way to save money on the initial purchase, as well as on the seeds from subsequent seasons. It doesn't take so much to get started, so it's never going to be a waste of money.

Buy healthy seed mix.

By using quality, well-loved plants and stems from your own garden for the seeds you buy, you can ensure an abundance of health and vitality in your new crops this season. It might be wise to buy more than one bag of seeds, so that you always have seeds available.

<u>Buy high-quality seeds.</u>

Always read the package of a seed bag before making a purchase, as they usually specify what kind of soil the plant is best suited for. Make sure that the proper amount of light and moisture goes along with any other conditions listed on the package. And if you're looking for a specific color or style of flower, then make sure to buy a package with those characteristics.

<u>Buy the best seeds for newer gardeners.</u>

If you're a beginner, and you don't have much experience planting a garden, then it's wise to buy seeds that are less vigorous. That way, you'll be able to make sure that they're healthy and free from disease, and they'll grow into strong plants rather than dying before they mature.

<u>Choose the right time of year to start seedlings.</u>

Plants have an ideal growing season, but this varies depending on the climate in which they're grown. Some plants can't grow well in summer heat, so it's better to start them in the winter. And if you aren't into gardening, then it's best to wait until spring or autumn before starting your seeds.

<u>Buy only parts of the plant.</u>

When you're at a nursery selecting your seeds, make sure to select only just one type of seed. If you buy all of the multiple types of seeds in a package, then there's no way that they'll all germinate successfully. And if one kind doesn't grow well, then most likely the others won't either.

Don't mix with another species.

Buy only seeds from your favorite plants that you want to grow. If you're not sure which seeds to choose, then read the package. Make sure that you've chosen the right varieties and don't mix your seeds with those of another species.

Buy only seedlings that are ready to be planted.

When selecting your seeds, make sure that the stems and plants are ready to be planted and germinated. If the seeds are still in their packaging, then they'll be too immature or still innumerous seeds so they won't root well.

Store your seedlings in a cool, dry location.

Seeds and seedlings are delicate, so it's not a good idea to put them in the fridge. If they do go into the fridge before you plant them, then they're likely to not germinate. Keep your seeds and young plants in a cool, dry place for several weeks before planting them.

Don't plant too early.

If you're starting your next garden to have some fresh tomatoes by June or July, then you'll be disappointed if it's still winter when you do that. The plants won't be able to handle the cold, nor will they be ready to harvest until later in the season.

Be patient.

Plants take a long time to mature. If you're starting a seedling for the first time, then expect it to take many weeks before it's ready to be planted outdoors. And if you don't have enough time in your schedule, then you can always make do without that new addition.

Don't use chemicals.

The soil in a garden is often the enemy of fresh plants. If you use chemicals to improve the quality of the soil, then you'll kill off the good bugs and help out the bad ones. So be choosy when buying seeds or plants at nurseries and avoid using chemicals to improve your soil in your garden.

Be cautious when buying from unknown suppliers.

If you want to buy seeds from someone other than a well-known seed company, then that person might not have any experience planting and growing your type of seeds successfully. They might not be able to offer you advice on how to best take care of your new plants, or they might scratch up your seeds or plants.

Be careful when buying plants at nurseries.

If you're buying plants at a nursery, then make sure that the plants aren't diseased. If the plants are diseased, then they might not grow well outside once you transplant them into the ground. Diseased plants also often carry diseases to other plants in your garden, so cut off any bad foliage from infected plants before moving them into your garden.

Don't buy seeds that are very old.

If you buy seeds that are past their expiration date, then those seeds will probably stop growing at some point. Or they might not grow at all. So use common sense when buying seeds. Don't buy old seeds that are over two years old or so.

Pick out the healthiest looking plants.

It's best to avoid picking out the plants with flowers or fruit on them because these plants are usually diseased and won't be that healthy after planting them into the ground or container garden.

Plant in a good quality potting soil.

If you're starting a new seedling, then look for one that looks healthy, has roots and healthy leaves. But if the plant has already seen plenty of sunlight and isn't still very small, then you can put it in regular garden soil.

Don't under-water young plants.

Young plants need adequate amounts of water to grow well. So don't always water them when they need it or when they show signs of thirst. Water them when they're thirsty and don't water them when they look healthy and strong.

These tips should help you have fruitful gardening on your own terms. You can do it without harming the environment too much.

What kind of plants do you need for your own garden?

As far as what kind of plants you need, that will depend on the type of garden you want to plant. If you want a large yard to grow your own produce or flowers, then you'll need some trees and shrubs. Of course, if it is a very small yard, then those won't be an option for your purposes.

If you're considering starting a garden at home, there are several factors to keep in mind while deciding what kinds of plants to grow. Some plants grow better in certain climates than others and not all plants are suitable for a small garden. You may want to choose from only compact plants that produce food in a small space or you may want to grow your own herbs.

Here are some of the plants that are popular for home gardens:

Tomatoes - Tomatoes come in many colors and ripen at different times, providing fresh tomatoes year-round. Plant your tomatoes in a later summer season so they can ripen during the cooler months.

Peppers - Peppers are a versatile garden vegetable that can be grown in pots on the patio, as well as in the ground. They come in different colors and shapes, including red, orange, yellow and purple.

Beans - Beans don't require much space to grow and they add vitamins A and C to your diet. Harvest your beans as they mature and you'll have a fresh supply of green beans, yellow wax beans or Italian flat beans.

Onions - Onions grow well in containers or small patches of soil near the house. They can be used in recipes to spice up meat, fish, soups and salads. Choose your favorite onions from red, white or yellow varieties.

Lettuce - Lettuce is easy to grow from seed in pots on the patio or in the ground around the house. It's a delicious leafy green that can be used fresh or in salads.

Garlic - Garlic is a versatile herb that can be grown just about anywhere indoors and outdoors. It helps the immune system by fighting bacteria and viruses as well as strengthening our blood. Garlic is also a natural mosquito repellant. Plant your garlic in containers or in the ground around the patio where you want to snuggle up next to it.

Carrots - Carrots can be grown in containers or in the ground around your home. If you use containers, you won't have to weed or use pesticides because you can bring them inside when it freezes.

Cucumbers - Cucumbers are a refreshing salad vegetable that grow well in small spaces and can be placed on the patio or in a pot. Like peppers, they come in many different colors and shapes. Check out the many types of cucumbers available at your local nursery for unique varieties.

Figs - Figs are a small tree that needs full sunshine to thrive. It's a hardy tree that provides delicious fruit for the whole family to enjoy. Plant your fig tree near the house for easy access and pick fresh figs from August-October.

Rhubarb - Rhubarb is a biennial plant that needs six months of cold weather in order to grow properly. It produces bright red stems that can be used as a garnish or cooked as vegetables. Plant your rhubarb in containers near the patio to keep it out of reach from pets and children.

What are some other types of plants you can grow?

Top fruit trees:

Pomegranate - These juicy fruits are a great source of vitamins A, B6 and C. The seeds are high in fiber and antioxidants. Different varieties ripen at different times so you can enjoy fresh pomegranates year-round.

Plums - Peaches, apricots and nectarines are commonly referred to as stone fruits. They are known for their juicy fruit and sweet flavor. You can eat the peaches whole, slice the apricots into segments or remove the pits and core them from nectarines to make delicious snack treats called "pits.

Peaches - Peaches are a popular fruit that can be eaten fresh, canned or cooked into sauces, pies and cobblers. They make a great snack between meals because they are sweet and delicious.

Apples - Apples can be eaten fresh as snacks or baked in treats like pies, cobblers and apple sauce. They are also used to be ingredients in some recipes, like apple juice, apple cider vinegar, apple jelly and applesauce.

Bananas - Bananas are another favorite snack food that's sweet and easy to eat. You can slice them into slices, mash them for banana bread or freeze them to make delicious frozen fruit pops.

Cherries - Cherries are a low-calorie fruit with a sweet flavor that can be eaten fresh or used in pies, cobblers and jams. Choose from dozens of different varieties of cherries available at your local nursery.

Strawberries - These berries are small but packed with flavor. You can eat them fresh, freeze them for future use or make a sauce from them.

Orange - Oranges are packed with vitamin C and provide a delicious source of vitamin C in your diet. Choose from several different types of oranges and enjoy their sweet flavor in fruit salads, cocktails and smoothies.

Fruits and Flowers By Season

Warm weather

This season is warm and sunny, which provides perfect conditions for planting fruits. This time your garden is for the summer months and you could plant strawberries, melons, peaches, cherries or blueberries.
It is also a great time to harvest lettuce and spinach which will mature into large leafy heads by the end of the summer.
This is a very good time to plant either ornamental flowers or vegetables such as carrots. Be sure you add a layer of mulch around the base of your plant to protect them from frost damage.

Cold weather

This season provides more cooling days that are perfect for planting flowers and vegetables.
You can plant potatoes; cabbage; cauliflower; broccoli; kale and lettuce in this season.
Start your crocus bulbs into the soil as soon as you can.
Crops that can be planted in this season include.
Strawberries, melons, peas, beans and apples.
Flowers that are suitable for planting in this season include.
Roses, lilies, peonies and geraniums.
You can also take cuttings of herbs during this season such as parsley, chives and sage.
Make sure you are keeping your garden tidy and free from weeds by weeding regularly.
If you do not have a large garden areas then start with a window box that you can place on the balcony or patio.

Humid climate

This season allows you to grow crops and vegetables throughout the winter months, for example; lettuce, cabbage and broccoli.
In this season gardeners can plant carrots; peppers and spinach.
Weed the garden biweekly to make it look neat.
Water your plants deeply but infrequently in this season. This helps them grow quickly and large in size.
Sprinkle evenly with all-purpose fertilizer at one-month intervals throughout the growing season using a blender or spreader.
Pansies, lilies and daffodils are also good to grow in this season.

Summer season

Plants to grow in this season include; sage, rosemary, parsley, chives and thyme.
They thrive well in the summer sun.
In this season you can plant tomatoes, peppers and lettuce.
Plant these vegetable crops after the last frost date.
It's important to keep a regular schedule watering your garden.
Use an automatic sprinkler.
Flowers that can also be planted in this season include nasturtiums and marigolds.

Plant flowers in late spring or after the last frost date.

Fall season

This is the best time to plant summer crops, including tomatoes, peppers, and squash.
The fall is the best time to plant and harvest potatoes.
Plant your seed potatoes into soil 3 to 4 weeks before you want them to be ready for harvest.
Your garden should have lush crops of fruits and vegetables throughout the summer months.
Fall season is the best time for you to harvest these crops.
Flowers that can also be planted in this season include pansies, marigolds, nasturtiums and verbena.
Watering your garden in the fall is important to help with plant growth.

Winter season

This is the best time to plant crops that are for the winter season.
You can plant parsnips, rutabagas, and turnips.
The winter season is a good time to plant crops that will mature in the spring-like lettuce, cabbage, and broccoli.
Flowers that can also be planted in this season are pansies, sweet alyssum and snapdragons.
Water at least once a week.
In a cold or freezing day, it is very important to water your garden thoroughly but ensure to do it early in the day. This will help keep your plant warm. If you have forecast, plant to water days before to prepare your plants for the freeze.
Fertilize your garden in the fall season using a balanced fertilizer at one-month intervals.
Your plants will grow quickly when it is warm and sunny, so you must keep them watered properly.
In this way, they will continue to grow and thrive throughout the summer months. You can enjoy the fruits and flowers of your labor for years to come with proper care and maintenance of your garden bed.

Tips on Starting A Home Gardening Business

Do you want to begin gardening at home but don't know how? It doesn't have to be difficult. You simply need the right information and some basic supplies.

First, determine what you wish to grow – vegetables or flowers. If it's vegetables, consider seeding three different types of plants: short season (60 days or less), long season (90-120 days) and a midseason variety (90-150 days). Flowers can be grown year round in most regions.

Another consideration is that certain plants are best grown during specific times of the year. Some are cool-season crops, while others are warm season. Cool-season crops should not be planted until the soil temperature reaches 60ºF. Warm season crops like broccoli and tomatoes should not be planted until nighttime temperatures are at least 45ºF.

Plan your garden to make the most of your available space; for example, plant in a staggered pattern, staggering the rows of each plant type (e.g. plant a row of carrots, then a row of beets, then a row of radishes). Having your garden in blocks rather than rows makes it easier to reach the center of the plant.

Mulching is also important in gardening. Mulch applied around plants helps retain moisture in your soil, prevents weeds, and keeps down insect populations.

Finally, pick appropriate seeds. If you buy seeds, read about the needs of the plant and purchase seeds accordingly. Starter plants are more expensive but can save time since they are already mature and ready to be transplanted into your garden. When choosing transplants, look for a healthy, uniformly colored plant with no soft or discolored spots. The stem should appear firm to the touch.

1. First, choose your space wisely

Your garden should be in an area that gets plenty of sunlight, but not be too exposed to wind or rain. Sometimes, what you need is a patch of space in between two fences or even on a balcony if you are lucky enough to have one. In any case, being able to grow your own vegetables is a great feeling and well worth the effort spent on it.

2. Start small

While you will obviously need to buy some gardening tools and seeds, there are some things that you could do on your own at home just by using the right materials and techniques. For instance, you could use soda bottles for watering them and even old newspapers for mulching plants. Make sure you get enough compost or manure as well so you can always amend the soil in your garden when necessary. In fact, with a little effort, your garden will be ready for planting very soon!

3. Become a pest control specialist

In order to grow any plants successfully and control pests which might cause plants harm or even death, there are certain techniques you should use. For instance, you could spray your garden with insecticidal soap or other organic products that are available in the market. You may also cover your plants with a layer of fine mesh to exclude pests from accessing them.

4. Control the weeds

Weeds are a common problem in any garden, especially if you are just starting out. The good news is that you can easily control them without using too much time or money on it. Mulching, using cardboard and other similar materials for creating weed barriers as well as implementing some other weed control methods should be enough to give you some time to relax while your plants grow.

5. Learn and practice

Finally, make sure you take the time to learn about your plants and how they should be watered, mulched and treated in every situation possible. Over time, you will get to know them so well that you will have a better chance of growing them successfully on your own. You can even consider taking some classes if you want professional advice.

Getting started in gardening business at home can be a bit daunting, if you are not sure where to start. If you want to get started quickly, the following six pointers will help you begin your green thumb career in no time.

1. Identify Your Goal

You first need to evaluate what kind of experience and knowledge you have before starting a gardening business at home. When you have never done any gardening before, it may be best to start with something smaller, like succulents or bonsai plants. Planting vegetables or herbs may be more time consuming, and you will want to be sure that you have enough time to tend to them.

2. Plan Ahead

Before you decide what type of plants you want in your
 gardening business at home, make a list of everything that you need. This is especially important if you are just starting out, and have no garden tools or equipment.

3. Select Your Plants

Next, start thinking about what plants you would like to grow. For a small startup business at home, it is best to stick with simple plants that do not require much upkeep. Many of these are very easy to keep alive, and will need watering every two weeks or so. Some examples include succulents, herbs and leafy greens.

4. Invest in Quality

When you are getting started, it is very important to invest in quality garden tools and equipment. Good supplies will save you so much time and energy that could be invested into growing your gardening business at home.

5. Spread the Word

Lastly, you will have to decide how you plan to promote your business. There are a lot of methods to do this, including social media, word of mouth or even online marketing. You can also print up some flyers or business cards and leave them with your neighbors. These are just few tips available in the idea of growing your own vegetables or flowers at home. Now, you can start your own home gardening business and start enjoying the great taste of fresh produce every day.

How do I start a micro-farming business?

Micro-farming is a form of sustainable agriculture that applies the principles of permaculture to smallholdings on a relatively small scale. Micro-farmers use organic methods, often on marginal land unsuitable for conventional farming or gardening. The goal is to produce fresh food and crops with minimal inputs such as water, soil, and fossil fuels. Permaculture focuses on achieving a self-sustaining system that does not deplete natural resources or cause pollution.

Micro-farming is often a form of urban horticulture practiced on vacant public land. Urban gardening differs from micro-farming in that urban gardening is usually carried out within the bounds of private lands, such as backyard gardens or allotments, and relies less on permaculture concepts.

Micro-farming can be seen as a form of worthwhile economic development for the community, providing food and employment, while enhancing self-sufficiency. In many countries, a high proportion of the population resides in rural areas but a large proportion of the GDP is generated by metropolitan economies. The conditions in both rural and urban areas have to be addressed in an integrated way to ensure food security. The urban micro farmers market sells its produce at farmer's markets and directly to local restaurants or shops that cater to organic, fresh produce. The market allows farmers to get their produce to the customer at a lower price and for consumers to know where they are getting their food from and the kind of food they are eating. The market places the consumer in contact with the producer and gives them information about how and where their food is produced. This also provides good marketing for farmers who may be producing more than what they can sell locally, which leads them to export their surplus produce or cultivate new consumers in areas they have never sold in before. Micro-farming as a profitable business venture is difficult in areas that are not densely populated with people. Many of the buyers for micro-farm produce are restaurants and organic food stores. The price for these goods is dictated by the market, which can be hard to control. The price a farmer gets for their goods has also been known to fluctuate depending on matters which don't have anything to do with the quality of their product, such as weather.

Start a micro-farm business

To start a micro-farm business, one must first decide on the type of farming they wish to enter into. The most common type of micro-farming is Urban Garden. These farms are either on land devoted to the purpose (e.g. a city park) or on vacant lots in urban areas that are not desirable for commercial farming. Urban gardeners build raised beds and compost, which simply means they store their organic waste products under plastic in garbage bins and turn them into soil that is rich in nutrients. Out of all the crops that can be grown, tomatoes are a very popular vegetable because of their health benefits, juicy flavor and short growing season with good cold hardiness. How to make it a business is to start off by selling your produce at farmer's markets or directly to restaurants.

are so many methods that can be used to start an Urban Garden with very little money. Many communities do not allow gardening on a private lot without the proper permits and zoning permissions. The initial step is to contact your local government and ask if there are any available plots for use as community gardens and if you can reserve one for yourself. The land you lease needs to be safe for gardening, which means it should not have sewage lines, electrical outlets or any other features that would harm the plants. Also, make sure there is enough light for your plants and you can take care of all the maintenance yourself.

The next step is to select your crops. The most popular crops are tomatoes and peppers. The first step is to upkeep the garden by preparing the soil with compost and fertilizer. Then you plant the seeds, depending on the season. In cooler weather, you want to use sprouted seeds, which are easily obtained from friends or family members who have gotten them before and believe in sustainable agriculture. After planting, you must tend to your garden regularly by watering it and removing debris.

Next, you can start selling your goods at farmer's markets or directly to local restaurants that specialize in locally grown organic produce. Many of these restaurants have "locally grown" signs on their front doors.

Urban gardening as a viable investment

Urban gardening has several advantages as a profitable business venture. Although urban farming is more labor-intensive than off-farm micro-farming, it can be relatively inexpensive to raise the required nutrients for producing crops, since much of an urban area's fertility and water has already been stripped from the soil by previous use. It can be challenging to produce high yields in small spaces, but the increased value of food grown in urban gardens often makes the effort worthwhile. Urban gardens are a good choice for gardeners who have limited access to land. For city dwellers, it is also a less disruptive alternative to commuting to rural areas for long hours of gardening or farming.

Urban gardening can supply most of the basic needs of its frequent users: fruits and vegetables, flowers and herbs; besides it gives also satisfaction which is missing in supermarkets - organic and seasonal products. This satisfaction can be expressed into a monetary value and may well compensate the efforts in cultivating a garden. Most of the food production in urban gardens is intended for personal use, but surplus can be sold either to neighbors or at farmers' markets. The latter option is particularly popular with community gardens. Neighborhoods with separate park areas can reserve them for urban gardening and, sometimes even for a fee, provide them with basic infrastructure such as soil and water supply, electricity. They can also provide basic amenities to the urban gardeners, such as benches and trash cans.

Growers of micro-farms often supplement their operations with a combination of on-farm sales (such as from the home garden) and off-farm sales (such as from farmer's markets). Some micro-farms only produce for personal use or for sale locally. Others specialize in selling through local farmer's markets, which can be a low-cost method of marketing products.

Micro farming is also an excellent business idea for people who want to get into farming but have limited funds to invest inland. Whether an acre or just a plot on your front lawn, micro farms can turn out profitable harvests with surprisingly little effort. Micro-farms are particularly helpful for those who live in apartment buildings or have rental properties.

Marketing strategies you can use for your Micro-farm Business

There are variety of methods to market your gardening company. Being creative with your marketing is key, and can be done in a number of ways. Below are some of the best ways you can market your business.

Making sure your marketing efforts are as varied as you can execute. This will make it more likely that people will see your company as a result of one or more marketing strategies.

Promoting your Micro-farm business

Promote a healthy lifestyle by teaching the benefits of eating fresh, organic produce. If you're starting an urban gardening company, give people a chance to learn about gardening. This can be done in a number of ways; whether it's teaching classes at the local community center, or even just offering basic gardening advice to people that are planting gardens outside of their own homes. By promoting the benefits of a fresh, healthy lifestyle you are more likely to stimulate business.

Promoting your gardening company as a local environmentally friendly business can also be a way to market your Micro-farm. If you're not only teaching the benefits of having a garden, but also showing people how it's better for them and the environment then it will help increase your client base.

Creative Marketing Strategies

If you're hosting an urban gardening service, then consider offering cooking classes and preparing meals using fresh produce from your garden. This could increase your client base and it could also help you to make money, which will help you to expand your business.

You may also market your business by offering classes in making organic, natural products. This can include things like soap, candles, laundry detergent and more. Whatever you decide, just make sure you're creating a strong marketing plan in order to increase your business.

E-Commerce

When you want an easy way to sell your products and services, then consider using the Internet as a way of creating the best possible Micro-farm.

You can use the Internet to sell gardening seeds, plant pots and even gardening equipment. You can also sell herbs and any other medicinal plants that are growing on your Micro-farm. You should be able to get all of this done through online shops. Online farmers' markets are also a good idea. When you market your products online, you can get an increase in business from people across the globe.

Just make sure that when you're planning your Micro-farm online store that you do it well. Having a website is very vital to attracting new customers, so make sure to include a lot of information about your business and the products that you sell.

Social Media

If you're using social media to promote your business and the Micro-Farm that you're running, then you should consider adding a Facebook page and a Twitter account. Take advantage of these social networks by posting updates about your business, customers, events and any other information that you think people would find useful. This can help you to increase your customer base as well as connect with new clients.

You could also use social media to educate people about the importance of having a garden. By educating them on the benefits of city gardening, you are more likely to increase your client base and also increase your profits.

With an effective marketing plan by your side, expanding your business will become easier. The more customers you have, the more profit you can make. Just remember that the

Another way to market your gardening company is to participate in local community events such as craft fairs and farmers' markets. Making a difference in your community is a great way to show people that your company and your products are worth investing in.

If you're hosting a gardening service, then consider giving your patrons the opportunity to take some of your organic produce home with them. This can help get you a great reputation and it can also help to increase your client base.

Most grocery stores sell organic foods, so if you're looking for another way to market your products online then consider selling them on online grocery websites as well.

You should also market yourself as an environmentally friendly company. By showing people the benefits of having a garden and sharing information about the benefits of eating fresh, organic produce then you can increase your profitability as well as customer base.

By taking all of these steps you will be able to market your business effectively and it will help to increase sales.

Just remember that the best way to get started in urban farming is to create an effective marketing plan. Once you're able to do this then you'll be able to grow your business in a big way!

Resources for Gardening

Gardening is a popular hobby for many of us, including both adults and children. It's not an easy hobby to master, but it can be quite rewarding and lead to beautiful results. We will tackle about some of the things you need to get started with gardening.

- Gardening Supplies: You are going to need a few tools that will help you cultivate your garden. Hire someone for this, or purchase what you need online or at the store. An easy way to get started with gardening is to purchase a couple of seeds and plants from your local nursery. The plant selection should include vegetables, herbs, roses and more. You could do a lot with just a few types of seeds and plants. Once you're ready to expand your garden, then go out and purchase the rest of the supplies in order for you to be productive.
- Most of the supplies you need for gardening can be purchased at your local home improvement store or online. There are many different options that you will want to purchase in order for you to have the tools necessary to begin your garden. Many of these items can also be found at garage sales and thrift stores.
- Gardening Seeds: In order to have a successful garden you are going to need to purchase some seeds. You may choose from a number of different vegetables, fruits and flowers when selecting from seeds. Some of the most popular seeds that people purchase include tomatoes, pepper & celery seed, spinach, corn and broccoli. It's important for you to research which type of seeds will grow best in your area. Most places that grow gardening products will have a pamphlet that you can refer to when purchasing seeds.
- Gardening seed companies are one of the best ways to get started in the world of gardening. While some gardeners are able to grow their own plants from seed, most of these people have experience in growing their own plants, so it is better for them. This way they know exactly what they're getting themselves into.
- Gardening Planting Plan: This is a great thing to have, and it will also help you get your garden started. You can easily find an example planting plan online or you can have someone from the store help you out with this. A planting plan illustrates where things are planted in the garden so that everything looks nice and neat once everything has grown. It also ensures that there is a good flow of energy throughout, encouraging the plants inside it to grow nicely and healthily.
- Garden Furniture: You are going to need somewhere to sit and enjoy your garden, so you might want to invest in some garden furniture. This is a great option for those who don't have the space indoors for an extra area. You can also use this as a nice place to store gardening tools and supplies during the off seasons.

There are many different types of garden furniture available from wooden chairs or benches, to metal chairs that feature canvas chairs or mesh chairs. Whether you're searching for an outdoor space to relax in and enjoy your gardening or you're looking for a piece of furniture which will stand out, garden furniture is a great option.

- Garden Tools: You are going to need some tools to help you finish your garden. Some of these include tiller, trimmers, scissors or secateurs. You may also find a great selection of hand tools such as hoes, rakes and shovels. When selecting your tools you should choose something that is going to be comfortable for you when in use. You want to be able to feel at ease with the tool and not have it tire your arm out. When in the store looking for garden tools try them out before you purchase if they have a carrying or testing area.
- Planters and Pots: Your plants are going to need somewhere to live, so investing in some planters and pots is important for them. Planters and pots can be made of ceramic, wood or metal. Some people even choose to use glass bottles to contain their plants indoors. The choice is up to you and based on your needs. You are also going to need a few different sizes of pots depending on the plants you are growing.
- Bedding Plants: These are usually flowers that can be purchased from a nursery or other garden store. They are easy to grow, so even beginners should be able to have some success. These can be planted in pots or in the garden. When planting in the garden you will have to add additional soil around these flowers so that they can grow larger than they do when first planted.

Some of the most popular bedding plants include marigolds, petunias and pansies. These are smaller plantings that you can add to your garden or put together as a flower bed at home. They are easy to grown and can help your garden look great all year round.

- Wildflowers: You may be able to find wildflowers growing in your area, but most people purchase these already grown. They are very attractive and may be used as border plants or as a centerpiece in the middle of your garden. These are a fun way to liven things up if you live in a colder climate that doesn't have a lot of greenery growing off season.

Where can you buy organic seeds and plants?

Having a beautiful garden can be one of life's greatest joys. But while the flowers look beautiful, they also need a little help in order to provide their own bountiful beauty. There are many places to buy organic seeds and plants. Most grocery stores carry at least a small selection of organic seeds. Farmers' markets are another wonderful option for finding organic seeds.

Contrary to popular belief, big box stores like Lowe's and Home Depot do not offer organic seeds or plants. They only carry hybrid or genetically modified (GM) varieties of plants. Seed diversity is limited as well, so you will probably have better luck finding what you need at the local farmer's market or nursery.

If that doesn't work, try a local garden center. However, most garden centers carry only hybrid varieties of plants and will not have any organic varieties.

Also, keep your eyes open for heirloom seeds and plants from local farmers at farmers markets, community gardens or even on roadside stands.

What do I need to get started?

Before you start any planting, research the types of crops and varieties that will grow best in your area. A few of the common plants and crops are listed below.

These are kid-friendly, do-able projects for gardeners of all ages. And, since many of these plants and crops require very little care, your kids can even help in their own garden!

You may want to note that some varieties of squash can vary in size, shape and color – so it is best to research what you are looking for before you purchase. Also, you can make note of what harvest times are ideal for your area. For example, in the middle of summer squash would not be ready for harvest – it would be too hot outside and squash likes to be harvested when the temperature has cooled down a little.

Although most of us think of spinach as a cool-season crop, it can tolerate heat well once established. Plant spinach seeds in a container, with just a pinch of fertilizer, about one month before the last frost date. It is the best to begin the plants indoors. Spinach plants often bolt (go to seed) shortly after they mature, especially if it is hot outside or if they are crowded.

What are the tips for making the most of your time gardening?

Have a plan! Before you plant, make a checklist so that you know which seeds and plants to purchase. It is better to buy too much seed than not enough. Also, be sure to take advantage of seasonal activities like National Garden Month (March) and National Gardening Month (mid-May).

How do I store my seeds and transplants?

Most seed packets contain detailed information about how long seeds will remain viable. They usually specify whether or not they need to be refrigerated, cold-stored, stored in a dark place etc.

Be sure to follow these instructions carefully. Also, if you have seeds that you would like to save for the next year, be sure to store them so that they will remain viable.

The cucumber plant has no special requirements for seed and transplant storage. However, squash plants are often very delicate so it is best not to store them inside. You may want to purchase some small pots and keep a few at home so that you can start some seedlings early; then put them out in the garden once the weather has settled down.

I have several banana plants. Should I save seeds from each, or should I be sure to preserve the last fruits?

Saving seeds from fruit that is sweet, ripe and firm (ripe fruit) is the best way to ensure that you have a plant for the next year. You don't want to save fruit that is still green and hard because the conditions for ripening may not be the same next year. Also, you may want to remember that fruits with more seeds often taste better than those with fewer. On the other hand, saving seeds from a plant that is starting to rot, ones that have already started to rot and those that are overripe are not as reliable.

When storing seeds, keep them at a cool temperature such as 60 degrees Fahrenheit, and don't let them sit near air conditioning vents. A dark place is also key for preserving the germination of squash seeds.

Be prepared! To ensure that you have a lot of time to plant your seedlings, be sure to purchase enough seedlings for your needs.

Gardening and how it helps with mental health, mindfulness and meditation

There's a lot of research to show how gardening and nature have an impact on mental health. There are some specific benefits of gardening that make it a great option for your mental health.

The act of gardening is known to produce relaxation in people, as well as reduce stress levels and blood pressure. There are several benefits to this practice which includes boosting your mood and lowering stress, improving air quality and increasing the biodiversity around you. The garden will cultivate richer soil through composting and provide additional income by growing food.

Gardening is an opportunity to take some time for yourself, and engage in a different activity that's low impact yet requires focus and attention. Boosting self-esteem and reducing depression can be another byproduct of gardening. This can provide physical exercise as well, which is one way to combat depression. Even if you don't feel like it when you first start, give it some time: You would notice a difference in how you are feeling after just a few weeks of regular activity in the garden.

Gardening may also be a form of meditation: It's been shown to decrease anxiety, improve concentration, memory and creativity. The noise and fast pace of many city environments can only add to feelings of stress and anxiety. Gardening can break up that cycle.

The mindfulness aspect of gardening is something anyone interested in meditation should try. It's a good way to learn about your need for quiet, and how you react to different stimuli in your home and garden environment.

If you're just starting out this can be hard, but try to hold onto one thought or feeling while you're gardening. Being aware of your feelings and judgments can be helpful in learning how to let go of racing thoughts and distractions.

While you're walking around your garden it can be a great time to take inventory of your thoughts and feelings as well. Always take note of how you may feel when you wake up, look around, do some weeding, or just sit down for a minute or two. Learn about yourself by observing these things. This can be a great time to do a little journal writing as well. Describe how you feel about your surroundings, what you think of, how it makes you feel.

This is important for anyone interested in meditation, mindfulness and improving mental health. It's easy to just relax by reading a book or listening to music, but gardening can be a calming activity while strengthening the mind at the same time.

Gardening is believed to be beneficial for aging adults and can keep the mind young. It's also a great activity for those with Alzheimer's or other types of dementia, as it can slow the progression of degenerative diseases.

Gardening is also an opportunity to create something beautiful. It's something you can take pride in and feel good about. It's a great asset in any home or business. Gardening is a positive, uplifting experience that can enrich anyone's life.

FAQs on gardening

Q: What do I need for a garden?
A: You'll need some good soil, seeds, plants, a few pots or containers to plant them in and finally some patience.
Q: What time of year may I start gardening?
A: Getting started earlier rather than later is typically recommended – the ground is more easily worked when it has had less exposure to frost and freezing temperatures. Generally, March marks the beginning of the growing season for most people.
Q: What should I grow?
A: Of course the most popular garden items are vegetables and fruits because people value their health and well-being. It's also fascinating to watch the progress of your plants as they grow; it's quite a rewarding experience. Gardening is also a significant activity for kids, adults, families or groups of friends – the possibilities are endless.
Q: I don't have much room for a garden, what can I grow in containers?
A: There is no set formula to follow for a container garden, but it does need to be something that you can water regularly. Popular items for a container garden are herbs (including basil and mint), flowers or hanging plants.
Q: What should I grow if I'm looking to add color or beauty?
A: Flowers are the most popular item in any garden. You can even make a small flower garden on the exterior of your house for spring, summer or fall.
Q: What are the benefits and enjoyment that I can get from gardening?
A: Gardening is an excellent exercise in patience and persistence – you will need to be with your plants every step of the way. The benefits include healthier plants, a chance to bond with your plants, learn about soil types and plant needs as well as a host of other benefits.
Q: I have a limited amount of time to spend on gardening, what are some of the most efficient plants to grow?
A: Some of the fastest growing vegetables and fruits include lettuce, radishes, spinach, tomatoes, cucumbers and strawberries. It's also recommended to grow taller vegetables such as beans or peas near the entrance to your garden so that you can easily pick them.
Q: How can I get my garden to look better all year round?
A: This is a good question and if you have a large area of land you can plant a variety of flowers to provide delight for everyone, not just in the spring and summer. Flowers such as cyclamen, poppies, daffodils and stock do well in containers. Year round interest can also be provided with bulbs such as tulips or hydrangeas.
Q: I'm a novice gardener, what does the process look like?
A: The process of gardening is essentially the same for everyone – start with good soil, make a seedbed and then plant your seeds. If you have not been successful in growing vegetables and fruits in your garden before you are advised to contact a local nursery or garden center for help.
Q: What should I do if I have plants that have died?
A: Plants that die can be dug up and planted in new soil. It's also possible to plant them in pots and use them as decoration. In most cases plants do not die on their own, it is usually pests or a disease that causes the plant's death.

Q: What should my garden look like?
A: The key to having a successful garden is balance and harmony – don't try to grow too many plants in one place, spread them out into small sections with enough space between each different type of plant for optimal growth.
Q: What are some tips for having a healthy garden?
A: One of the most important aspects of gardening is maintenance. Keep up with watering, fertilizing and weeding to keep your garden healthy. Look after your lawns and walkways; if you have a flower garden this is also important as a layer of sand can provide the moisture your plants need in order to thrive.
Q: What are the basic materials needed to build a garden?
A: The basic materials needed for building a garden can range from wood, stones, fountains and waterfalls. If you want to make a stone path you will need crushed gravel and cement. It's possible that you might also want to include some plants – flowers are always a good choice.
Q: What are some great ideas for making my garden look better?
A: There are many ways to make your garden look better. One of the most common ideas is to add a waterfall. Waterfalls can be made out of various materials including metal, rock and water.
Q: Is it possible to create an outdoor flower garden?
A: Yes – it's possible to have a flower garden outside your house. This is a great idea for spring, summer or fall and will bring beauty and color into your home with its blooms.
Q: What are some natural materials that I can use to make a garden?
A: You can use many different materials to create a gorgeous garden. For starters you can look around your property and see what you have available. This might include trees, rocks or even fallen branches or leaves that are rotting.
Q: What are some fun and unique ideas for making a garden?
A: One of the best ways to make your garden stand out is to do something different that is not traditional. It could be a good idea to grow plants that look different or include an interesting statue.
Q: What are the best materials for constructing a garden?
A: Depending on your needs and the type of garden you want to build, you might want to use anything from stone, metal or wood. It's a good idea to look at your home and see what materials are available. For example you can build the foundations of a stone garden using stones from your property or even locate buildings that have fallen down and use these stones.
Q: Is Organic gardening important?
A: Organic gardening is a way of growing or producing food that uses natural methods. This means there are no pesticides, synthetic fertilizers or genetically modified products involved.
Q: What are some tips for using organic materials in my garden?
A: It's possible to use all kinds of organic materials in your garden. Some examples include worm castings, plant clippings and even animal manure. As long as you are using natural products you will be able to grow a beautiful organic garden.
Q: What are some tips for making a potted plant?

A: Potted plants can add beauty and life to your home or garden. A great way to do this is to look around your property and see what you have that might work well for potted flowers, herbs or woody plants. Look at plants that have died and see if you can use their roots in a pot. As long as it's a living plant you will be able to grow new ones from the roots of the old one.

These are few questions that will help you learn more about gardening. Next time you are out, take some time to look around for plants that could grow well in your garden. The most essential matter to remember is that everyone's situation is different. Finding what works best for your yard and lifestyle is the key to making sure that your gardening is sustainable.

Is my backyard too small for a garden?

One advantage of gardening is that you don't need a backyard to get started. Your planting area can be as big or as small as your home or apartment's available space.
A small garden can yield more food per square foot than a large garden, and it's easier to manage because the variety of plants is less diverse. However, with a large garden you're able to grow more food varieties and have greater fun experimenting with different soil types, gardening methods, harvesting times and yields. If you have enough room for a large garden, it's a great idea to plant all your favorite food crops.
Need more space?
Besides growing lettuce or tomatoes, there are some plants you can grow even in small spaces, such as strawberries. Some varieties can even give you an edible harvest right off the plant. You can also make accessories to use on a smaller scale.
You're also able to have some really neat-looking gardening setups in small spaces. For example, with just a packet of peat moss, some seeds and Styrofoam cups you can make very realistic looking gardens that are fun to care for.

Can I start organic gardening at home?

Surprisingly, yes! It's never been easier to start an organic garden in your home. You can grow most of the vegetables and herbs you need on a small plot of ground without using any chemicals or other heavy-duty gardening products. This is a great way to cut down on the chemicals you and your family are exposed to in your daily lives.
Buying organic produce at the local store can get expensive, which is why it's even more worthwhile to grow it yourself. You can customize your organic garden based on your climate and what you like to eat.
People have been using chemicals for years in lawn care, and we're seeing the effects now. Many children are born with asthma and other allergic disorders because of these chemicals that are used on a daily basis. You can avoid these issues when you grow your own vegetables and fruits.

If you live in an area where you have a short growing season, or poor soil quality, then organic gardening may not be a good option for you. Try to find a local nursery or farm that sells organic plants that can grow into your climate and ecosystem. Making your own organic garden in a small space is also economical, fun, and rewarding.

Conclusion

Gardens are a great way to understand nature and the world around you. They provide us with a beautiful space to enjoy friends, family, and life's simple pleasures. Growing our own food can be an enlightening endeavor, but it can also be very rewarding as well. Gardening is considered by many a beneficial and relaxing hobby. It may be considered an activity for the whole family or a personal pursuit, by a gardener who enjoys it in their backyard with help of family members or alone. Gardening may be seen as a way to get some exercise and enjoy fresh air and open spaces, while getting some work done. Gardeners who have enough space and choose to grow plants for food can potentially produce food for themselves or for their loved ones. They can, thus, enjoy the health benefits associated with fresh, chemical-free food grown in their own organic garden. Gardening is also a way to have some exercise outdoors and breathe fresh air. Additionally, it is an enjoyable activity that can be done by all members of the family from toddlers to seniors. Furthermore, gardening helps homeowners save money on groceries and can be a fun family activity.

So whether you desire to grow a few vegetables for your family or produce enough food to feed all of your neighbors, now is the time to start a garden. City-dwellers have been slow taking up the gardening movement, but we encourage you to take a chance on this fresh new way of living. Vegetables are inexpensive and easy to grow!

Gardening is one of the best things that you can do for yourself as well as those around you. This is an act of love for the earth, your community and for your own health. Those who have started gardens have never looked back. Your life would change for the better. Just remember every time you plant a seed and water your garden, you are blessing those around you.

In terms of maintaining health, gardening has a lot of benefits. It makes it easier for gardeners to embrace healthy eating as they are growing most of their own food. Gardening is also very good exercise as gardeners are working in their yard either by digging, cutting, hoeing, watering, pulling weeds or planting. Gardening may also prolong the life expectancy of individuals and reduce risk of developing illnesses such as cancer because of the healthy balance it brings both physically, emotionally and especially mentally.

Thank you for reading this book and if you know someone who needs basic gardening advice and wants to start out in gardening, suggest please suggest this book!

Resources

Gilmer, M. (2003). Complete Idiot's Guide to a Beautiful Lawn (The Complete Idiot's Guide). Alpha.

How To Plant an urban garden:step by step tutorial. (2016). Fast Company. https://www.fastcompany.com/3058602/how-to-plant-an-urban-garden-a-step-by-step-tutorial

Urban Gardening For Beginners. (2021). Eco-Spotlight. https://eco-spotlight.com/feature/urban-gardening-for-beginners

Urban gardening supplies-tools for starting a community garden. (n.d.). Gardening Know How. https://www.gardeningknowhow.com/special/urban/urban-gardening-supplies.htm

Urban Gardening: The Ultimate Guide to City Gardening. (n.d.). Gardening Know How. https://www.gardeningknowhow.com/special/urban/urban-gardening-ultimate-guide.htm

www.ingramcontent.com/pod-product-compliance
Lightning Source LLC
Chambersburg PA
CBHW081622100526
44590CB00021B/3562